AMERICA WITHOUT ETHNICITY

Kennikat Press
National University Publications
Interdisciplinary Urban Series

Advisory Editor
Raymond A. Mohl

AMERICA

WITHOUT ETHNICITY

GORDON DANIEL MORGAN

National University Publications
KENNIKAT PRESS // 1981
Port Washington, N.Y. // London

*I am happy to dedicate this work
to all those who believe in the oneness
of America and who know, as the
writer does, that without this concept
America itself cannot exist.*

Manufactured in the United States of America

Published by
Kennikat Press Corp.
Port Washington, N.Y. / London

Library of Congress Cataloging in Publication Data

Morgan, Gordon Daniel.
    America without ethnicity.

    (Interdisciplinary urban series)
    Bibliography: p.
    Includes index.
        1. United States—Ethnic relations. 2. United
States—Race relations. 3. Pluralism (Social
sciences) 4. Minorities—United States. I. Title.
II. Series.
E184.A1M673   305.8'00973   81-18565
ISBN 0-8046-9293-9   AACR2

CONTENTS

ACKNOWLEDGMENTS

I wish to thank my wife, Izola, for lending support and a critical ear. She knows better than others, I believe, the importance of de-ethnicizing America. John Parke has also been a tremendous help. I am indebted to him for his criticism and encouragement. I also thank the many students who have listened to and reacted to my lectures and ideas which make up parts of this book.

AMERICA WITHOUT ETHNICITY

ABOUT THE AUTHOR

Gordon Daniel Morgan is a professor of sociology at the University of Arkansas. He holds a Ph.D. from Washington State University. He has received grants and awards in his field, and has served as a consultant to conferences and programs on the underprivileged, on ghetto students, and on improving human relations in problem cities.

1

INTRODUCTION

This book evolved out of an attempt to question cultural pluralism, a doctrine advocated and practiced by some academic men and women. College campuses have adopted the idea, and activities are increasingly separated by race and ethnicity. There appear to be fewer and fewer persons inclined to protest this trend and those who do are told that pluralism is the direction in which American society is moving. And unlike in the 1960s, the issue of segregated activities seldom arises. In the schools, administrators seem more willing to fund separate activities for racial and ethnic groups, leading to great fragmentation of campuses.

If there were a single event which sensitized the writer to the growing separation of the racial groups, it was the formation, around 1970, of the Black Caucus of the American Sociological Association. The caucus was begun in the wake of the murder of Martin Luther King, Jr., and as a reaction to the irrelevancy of mainstream sociology to the needs of the black and poor constituency, who are often the subjects of study. Many members felt that by pulling away from the main body they would achieve greater recognition and negotiate a better deal for black faculty and staff on campuses across the country. Tenure for younger black scholars was a burning issue at a time when many schools were facing hard financial choices brought about by declining enrollment, erosion of endowments, and loss of income.

The caucus tried to bring black sociologists together to reach some of the goals viewed as important to them and to the profession. After a few years of threatened disruption of meetings, running of candidates for office, and other political activity, the caucus became recognized as a subgroup of the general association. While blacks met separately, the association went on as usual. It was easier to make decisions since blacks had now retired to their separate caucus.

In some regional and state associations similar caucuses were formed. Other disciplines and fields in which blacks were well-represented, law enforcement, nursing, teaching, real estate, for example, began to see the emergence of black caucuses. Although they went by different names, they continued with the same evident purposes.

It soon became clear that young blacks were separating from the larger associations because they were afraid. Many did not have safe positions; some were, or felt they were, tokens used to satisfy affirmative action requirements. In the academic community, threats, implicit or actual, by some departments to remove blacks for allegations of nonproductivity kept blacks meeting to discover ways of confronting the employers upon whom they depended but over whom they had no control. Blacks reacted with the formation of caucuses to deal with group concerns. Their separation was a defensive reaction born of perceived threats to their security.

At first the separation of blacks within the various associations was considered something of an interesting fad. It was mysterious and unnerving to see all-white sessions while blacks were barricaded in other rooms. No one knew what the blacks were doing. Would they march and disrupt sessions as they had occasionally done in the past? Would they take some association official hostage and hold him until he agreed to nominate a black for president, then recommend he be accepted by acclamation? When the blacks failed to produce excitement, the women took their place, threatening to demonstrate for the same gains and goals for which blacks had protested. Chicano, Oriental, and Slavic caucuses soon got under way, though they made fewer headlines than blacks and women.

When asked about their separation, the various group representatives gave vague responses about the emerging concept of pluralism. This concept sounded better than segregation, for it seemed to be an option chosen by the group and not imposed upon it. But all the caucuses were based on the insecurity of members in their positions.

In the fall of 1976 the First National Black Think Tank was convened at the University of Maryland, College Park where I presented a paper entitled "Questioning Cultural Pluralism." I began thinking more seriously about cultural pluralism and added to my notes as I researched and wrote. My institution, the University of Arkansas, asked me later to give a public lecture from the perspective of my discipline in recognition of the bicentennial of America. The lecture was to be given in February of 1977 and my topic was "Sociology and Americanization Process

Theory." Preparation for this lecture enabled me to think seriously about the making of the American culture. I concluded that America is a culture in transition, moving toward equality, fair play, education, leisure, and prosperity. I could not imagine pluralism as viable in the long run for the country. I wanted to know why there had come to be such a leaning toward pluralism when it had hardly been considered in the early part of the century, a time when nearly all aspects of American life were opened up to allow greater participation of all citizens.

With resegregation occurring in the professional meetings, the time was ripe, it seemed, to examine the foundation of the doctrine of pluralism. But there are few neatly separated cultural groups in America. Most old Americans, including the nonreservation native Americans, have long since melted culturally. Could pluralism mean ethnic separation, an old phenomenon wrapped up in new clothes?

Cultural pluralism was used in various ways to cover linguistic, religious, national, ethnic, and many other subcultures, including racial groups. America has never shown a great deal of interest in cultural groups with slightly different habits and lifestyles. The only recognized groups have been blacks and whites. Culture has not mattered that much. Nearly all the groups were quite similar culturally, or were obviously becoming so. The ethnic group became the vehicle for the preservation of different cultures. But since the cultures were so similar there arose the use of the idea of race to keep groups separate. In America, culture and class would keep whites divided among themselves, with race the dividing line between blacks and whites. But cultural pluralism and ethnicity cannot be separated, and people of the same culture but of different ethnicity, race, or class are discouraged from all but superficial association.

Study revealed that the proponents of pluralism were growing in number and some scholars who were formerly known integrationists had shifted over to become pluralists. Much data and many conclusions seemed reflective of their philosophies regarding their own superiority and the inferiority of other people. It was not unlike 1927 when thirty-four distinguished scientists, mostly from Harvard and Yale, argued to protect superior Anglo-Saxon and northern European blood by restrictive immigration.[1] Today, the leading thought in support of cultural pluralism seems to emanate from three great learning centers: Harvard-MIT in the East, the University of Chicago in the Midwest, and Berkeley-Stanford in the West. As vertex schools of a learning-influence triangle imposed upon the U.S., these schools have a disproportionate influence on the direction of nearly all consequential social, scientific, and economic sectors of American life. Each center has its satellite institutions, and the larger of the satellite schools have their subsatellites. They are all integrated in such a way as to follow the lead of the major schools in their spheres. Only the top schools in the country are allowed to be truly innovative either in thought or actual research. The vertex schools have very little competition. Some non-vertex schools are outstanding in some fields and there are some excellent faculty in each school, but their numbers and influence are small. In general, the most important scholarship comes from the schools of the vertices.

In the social sciences, schools of the vertices have lately produced the most conservative scholarship. Their human relationships scholarship is especially conservative. At Harvard the work of Daniel P. Moynihan and Nathan Glazer is notable *(Beyond the Melting Pot)*. Edward Wilson's *Sociobiology* and Christopher Jencks's *Inequality* are in the conservative vein. At Chicago James Coleman's reinterpretation of his own data in the massive *Coleman Report* has caused him to conclude that busing does not have the merit he thought it had. He thus gives aid and comfort to the racist element which seeks theoretical justification in the conservative scholarship of major thinkers. In the West, Arthur Jensen's attack upon the abilities of black people became serious enough to cause racial rifts that may be years in healing.[2]

There are individuals, even in these vertex schools, who challenge the writings of the conservative scholars, but their voices are drowned out by those with greater "professional" support. Yet the most influential work, which sets the direction of American social development, comes from schools of the vertices. Such work is diverting America from its long and tortuous course toward human equality.

Ethnic change theories promulgated by American scholarship fall on a continuum, conceptually, from separatism to amalgamation or melting pot.[3] Under separatism, groups would have very little to do with each other and would retain their disparate institutional structures. This separation would probably be called cultural pluralism. This philosophy calls for the preservation of communal life, significant portions of the culture of diverse groups within the context of American citizenship, and political and economic integration into American society.

In this book my intention is to examine the logic behind the pluralist concept, to understand its origins and function, and to comment upon what appear to be its consequences for American society. In so doing I shall also examine its antithesis, the melting pot, which has come under attack within the past decade by significant elements of the academic community.

Writing this book has not been an easy task. It is based on my longstanding belief in the viability of America as a concept representing the promise of freedom for the indigenous millions and for the rest of the world. I was in Uganda when President Kennedy was struck down by an assassin's bullet. The poor people of that proud little country wept openly when they received the news. Somehow John Kennedy, himself the offspring of immigrants, represented the hope of people everywhere, the hope that the dream of equality and freedom would not die in America, for it was the only place left where these concepts had a real chance to reach fruition. The snuffing out of that brief candle killed a little bit more the belief that equality and freedom were possible anywhere in the world. Elsewhere abroad I saw young and old people walk a little straighter, prouder, more hopeful upon seeing an official vehicle come by displaying even a small American flag. In Scandinavia in 1975, when I was studying their criminal justice system, I saw people from various European countries, most of whom had never been to America, celebrate the Fourth of July with greater feeling and more tears than I ever witnessed or read about in the U.S.

For years I have wanted to understand the mystique of America. From the many articles and books I have read on its national character, what stood out in my mind was its idea of the equality of mankind. Its failure to implement this has important consequences for the people.

Somewhere in the 1950s things began to change. Black people got tired of going to the back of the bus. They refused to define themselves, or to be defined, any longer as odd men out. They had labored as diligently as any other group to build the prosperity of the country and would be double damned if inequities continued without redress.

America was not ready for the change. But the poor people of the world formed a psychological bond with the blacks and offered little support for America in their homelands so long as she aided unfairness through the gross mistreatment of her own minorities. American embassies were bombed, ships were captured, planes hijacked, diplomats held hostage. Everywhere the one country which stood for freedom was being named as the greatest obstructor of freedom. Frightened by the riots of the late1960s, and believing force would solve social problems, America turned its soldiers against the students of several colleges, killing and wounding them as in a fascist state. It jailed, on the slightest pretext, prominent people who disagreed with its poor foreign or domestic policies and built illegal dossiers on persons known for their loyalty to and unceasing fight for human justice. And it persisted far too long in a useless war which treated the lives of young men as cannon fodder and as guinea pigs for Agent Orange which covered the Vietnam jungles and countryside. War lords dressed in blue pin-striped suits gathered around the Capitol and White House. Anxious to make money and secure places in the history books, they traded the basic honor of the country for messes of political pottage.

In a few short presidential years America had earned the enmity of most of the nations of the Second and Third worlds, and even its Western allies would have defected if they were not trapped by some of the same contradictions that plagued America. By 1980 no nation gave a damn about America, and most wished it ill. America lost in Vietnam, lost East Africa, the Caribbean islands; and its frustrated leadership nervously fingered buttons which, if pushed, would embroil the world in the third great holocaust of the twentieth century. Small troubles with small countries became crises threatening world security. Its domestic policy lay in rack and ruin; the people were not only disgruntled, but pessimistic about a turn around.

America has not wished to examine itself. It externalizes its problems Archie Bunker-like. It's the Jews, the coloreds, or the communists. The stage has been set for some time for the emergence of leaders trying to define America by its division into various ethnic families. Others are to be excluded altogether so they may be scapegoats for its failure.

There have long been the Nazis of Skokie, Illinois, the Ku Klux Klan, the separatism of the Black Muslims, the Jewish Defense League, the White Citizens councils of the South, the academy movement, the ethnic vigilantes of Newark, and the numerous nativist and hate groups which spring up in the interstices of mass society. But somewhere there has always been the belief that these are not the groups and programs that would save America. Neither have Americans believed that an animal can ease its hunger by chewing off its own leg. But their fears have created space for the pluralists to operate, for they have not caught the vision and hope of "One America." The strength of the country has been its ability to rally 'round the concepts of fairness and equality. Pluralists would sap that strength by dividing the country into a variety of subnations with neither peace, strength, nor freedom.

The emphasis on cultural pluralism in America is rather recent. Writings on the topic are neither systematic nor tightly organized. They are seldom research findings but are largely hortatory appeals made by various authorities for the general public, including students. Pluralism is an historical reality but without demonstrated positive consequences for American society. Though pluralism may serve to unify small groups in a foreign country, it would certainly fractionalize American society. Here the emphasis has been on molding a large general culture around a few basic values rather than on many small, loosely-integrated ethnocentric cultures.

The defense of pluralism as an intellectual concept rests on proving that groups ought to be separate. A common view is to assert "chosenness" or "specialness." Intellectuals have asserted the chosenness of their group since about the fifteenth century, but scientists are unable to show the natural separation of mankind into races. Close examination has shown all differences between races to be fictitious, resolving into bell-shaped data curves whose tails overlap when all are placed on common continua. Force supplanted evolution in the form of slavery in the Americas to maintain the separation of mankind. The colonial experience of Africa and much of the Orient resulted from the application of naked force. The Germans paid a fantastic price to learn the lesson of the illogic of the "chosenness"-equals-superiority proposition, having their country destroyed twice in a thirty-year span. The jingoism of the Japanese and their frustration with the failure of their "superiority" to be translated into empire confused their leaders into thinking they could take over what the world had come to recognize as the sleeping giant guardian of human freedom. Their attack on Pearl Harbor sealed forever the doom of the idea of pluralism based on the pretensions of racial superiority. The total experience of the holocaust of World War 2 was enough to convince sensible people everywhere of the danger of the myth of "chosenness," whether this special status is considered the result of a Darwinian struggle for existence or a grant from God.

All groups with active historians and intellectuals have managed to position themselves at the center of world history, in the middle of a group of concentric circles. Other people are less worthy and centrifuge from the core. "We are different; we are chosen; we are special," say the centrists, creating a hiatus within the ranks of mankind. If one group is chosen, unchosen people must be damned. The myth is carried as if it were truth, and soon many begin to believe it. Once a myth of "chosenness" is set in place, evidence is not required to uphold it.

In this study I have tried to understand why there has been an attack on the melting pot. It was the social philosophy of most of the American population from its founding as a nation but was not always put into practice. There did not seem to be a basic shift in the attitudes of the public, but academics, many of whom had previously strongly supported the melting pot, began to advocate pluralism. Funds became available for pluralism studies and conferences while few funds were used to promote the melting pot. Ethnic manipulators used the federal government as a major source of funding. Some of these manipulators were soon upgraded to become ethnic bureaucrats who organize and oversee programs involving this or that special ethnic group. Sensing the mood of the country, manipulators and philosophers arose in every ethnic group to propagandize the beauty of ethnicity. Presidents played the ethnic theme, and concepts like "ethnic purity," and the "neighborhood school" became shorthand for the segregation of peoples. In schools and colleges ethnic studies proliferated, and students separated into enclaves.

Pluralism, ethnic and cultural, has now become a social movement with an ideology and structure to give it respectability. It has become the theoretical focus around which much thought has coalesced. There were and are persons who argued against the idea, but it has been most difficult to make headway against the waves of money and influence which support it. Its growth has been like a damburst whose water sweeps away everything in its path.

I have tried to understand what is disagreeable about the philosophy of the melting pot and have discovered that cultural and ethnic pluralism as currently advocated are divisive. Pluralistic cultures have been in existence in other countries for centuries. These countries seem so fragmented and weak that they could not be used as models for America. Pluralism means ethnic differences in other societies, but in America ethnicity and race are confused. Historically, America's recognition of ethnicity and pluralism has been weak, while its recognition of race has been strong. Ethnics had to be lumped with one or the other of two groups treated politically as races: blacks and whites. But even through times of great political corruption and uncertainty for groups outside the system, there remained general confidence in the ability of the country to command the loyalty of diverse peoples. America was a new opportunity structure, requiring a new personality to be successful in it. The mentality of the Old World would not work here.

All cultures require of their most successful citizens a certain degree of loyalty, independence, frugality, and technical skills. What America required, and other cultures did not, was a leveling of ascriptive status characteristics so that all might seek status from relatively equal starting positions. And even with respect to the very rich and very poor, placement by ascription has never been the norm in America. In philosophy, and increasingly in practice, all social positions, neighborhoods, and opportunities are open to all qualified contenders. Background is becoming less of a barrier to acquisition of the best style of living the country has to offer.

There are those who feel that the pluralism of culture, ethnicity, and race may be replaced by the pluralism of social class.[4] Such analyses usually ignore that class pluralism is no more acceptable to the American people than that of ethnicity and race. The American culture has not adopted class differences as part of its ideology.

America is at a social and cultural crossroads. The direction it takes will set the tone of social life for years to come. Following any path which diminishes the contacts of peoples will erode its strength, which resides in the absence of social barriers to personal achievement. The world is watching to see if America is willing to hold fast to its commitment to the equality of men; to reduce artificial and ascriptive obstacles to achievement. Writing this book, and allied papers not published herein, has enabled the writer to understand more clearly perhaps than most the long range and divisive consequences of the revival and continuity of ethnicity, which seems to be bootlegged under the cover of cultural pluralism. I hope that the public at large will scrutinize the implications of any form of pluralism before it is uncritically accepted as a program for the nation.

The first three chapters examine trends undermining the melting pot philosophy and establishing the plausibility of pluralism as an alternative practice and concept. In chapters 4 and 5 I try to uncover the underlying logic of pluralism while arguing that the melting pot prevails in spite of much recent talk about the vitality of pluralism. Chapters 6, 7, and 8 are concerned with pluralism as it exists in practice with some attention paid to its consequence for community life. Chapter 9 is concerned with how separatism emerged as a concept in the academic social sciences and how it became a foundation for advocacy in real life. Chapter 10 discusses political and cultural pluralism in comparative terms. The schools have been instrumental in promulgating the idea of pluralism; chapter 11 discusses the devolution of this role on the institutions of learning. In chapter 12 a study of textbooks reveals the process of inclusion of cultural pluralism discussion in general sociology textbooks. The depluralization of blacks and their retention of faith in assimilationist ideology and the meaning of their choice for other ethnic groups is discussed in chapter 13.

Finally, there are concluding remarks which summarize the general thesis of the book with the author's impressions of the meanings and implications of pluralism and ethnicity for America.

2

ATTACKS ON THE MELTING POT

Even though there have always been people who opposed the integration of different groups into American life, their numbers and influence have, until recently, been small compared to the large group tolerant of unified diversity. The concept of the melting pot has been promoted under different favorable names, such as Americanization, naturalization, assimilation, and amalgamation. These terms can be viewed as roughly synonymous since each means giving up Old World loyalties to become part of a new social and cultural system. The melting pot viewpoint suggests that groups, however different, will all be thrown together into the giant crucible of Americanization where, through the social processes, they will form one group and Old World hatreds, memories, and group prejudices will become meaningless.

Americanization implies eligibility for model citizenship, untainted by scandal or misconduct. It implies political patriotism. Religiously, it requires a Judaeo-Christian upbringing. Economically, it opens the way to a middle class lifestyle or above. Educationally, it means a college degree or aspiration thereto. Psychologically, it means and bestows freedom of thought and action. It is a process by which one moves ever closer to the ideals of fair play, human equality, dignity, and prosperity. Naturalization is the attainment of citizenship through a process other than birth to American citizens or on American soil. No less is expected of the naturalized citizen than of born Americans when it comes to the meeting of widely held norms defining Americans.

Assimilation is the process by which divergent groups come together to form a single and common way of life. The minority will lose its identity by absorption into the majority group, or two different groups will merge to become one. Amalgamation is the loss of identity through intermarriage among groups which are of different origin.

Most authorities agree that the predominant theory of immigrant socialization, up to near the end of the nineteenth century, was the melting pot. They argue that northern Europeans were the groups most successful in following this process. Groups comprising the "New Immigration," coming after the 1880s, experienced difficulty and many were considered unmeltable.

The melting pot has been assaulted on various fronts by different forces. The earliest attacks were in the form of objections to immigration. After the American Revolution opposition to immigration arose, but there was little clarification of the philosophy of ethnic relations. The Americans did not want the burden of maintaining poor people, regardless of their origin. The culture of the immigrant was not the issue in these early objections, for the majority of the immigrants were from the British Isles or western Europe and would themselves be quite assimilable.

Both George Washington and Thomas Jefferson had reservations about too free an immigration policy. Washington told John Adams in 1794: "My opinion, with respect to immigration, is that except of useful mechanics and some particular descriptions of men or professions, there is no need of encouragement...."[1] By 1836 Senator John Davis of Massachusetts was asking:

Is it morally right for Great Britain to attempt to throw upon us this oppressive burden of sustaining her poor? Shall she be permitted to legislate them out of the kingdom, and to impose upon us a tax for their support, without an effort on our part to countervail such a policy? ... Shall we fold our arms and see this moral pestilence sent among us to poison the public mind and do irremediable mischief?[2]

Of course Davis was referring to the undesirables from the alms-houses and prisons of England. Whether politicians were reacting to popular pressure regarding immigration, or were causing such pressures, is not well known. Gordon states: "The fruits of these fears in their extreme form were the Native American movement of the 1830s and 1840s with their anti-Catholic campaigns and their demands for restrictive naturalization and immigration laws and for keeping the foreign-born out of political office."

The period of the Civil War served to subdue the emphasis on restrictive immigration, and it was not until about the early 1880s that Congress moved to select who might come to the United States by excluding lunatics, idiots, convicts (except those convicted of political offenses), and persons likely to become a public charge.[3]

Labor unrest in the 1880s led native-born whites to press for legis-lation excluding the importation of contract labor from abroad. Groups such as the American Protective Association, largely anti-Catholic, campaigned against the Irish, but also objected to the immigrants coming in large numbers from Italy, Russia, Austria-Hungary, and the Balkans.[4]

The antiimmigration programs of the late 1880s, in a sense, struck against the melting pot by making it more difficult for "unassimilable" people to enter the country. The main objection was their poverty. This was often connected with their religion—mainly Catholic—not their color. As long as the newcomers were few in number, those who were in the country were more easily integrated into the mainstream of society.

While debates were raging in the East over the question of European immigration, in the West a similar issue was being raised concerning Orientals. Agitation against Orientals continued from about the early 1880s (there was anti-Chinese sentiment even before) into the twentieth century. By 1906 Oriental restaurants were boycotted, their managers and customers beaten, their property destroyed, and their owners forced to pay for protection. Japanese, Chinese, and Korean children in San Francisco were required to attend a school for Orientals. At first this anti-Oriental sentiment was localized on the West Coast, but later it spread to the rest of the country.[5]

Madison Grant's *The Passing of the Great Race* came at a propitious time, 1916, and argued against the dilution of superior Anglo-Saxon blood through mixing with the inferior peoples of southern and eastern Europe and elsewhere. By the mid-1920s the national origins system of admitting quotas of persons from various countries in proportion to the estimates of their numbers already in the U. S. was in effect.

Detractors of the melting pot position claim that people excluded may not be assimilable, which is a bit different from saying that those already in the culture can never become assimilated. Probably few persons recognize that the antiimmigration legislation did not neces-sarily reflect any objection by the general public to the presence of immi-grants whose lifestyles and values differed from those already in America.

Once the political attack was made on the melting pot, it became relatively easy for academics to take up the chant. Their agreement with the politics of separation is understandable in view of academic tendencies to conform their ideas to what they perceive as political reality. Quite often scholars may not be aware of their subliminal needs to find agree-ment with the politics of the times. The consequences of university scholars acquiescing to political dogma can be seen in the case of Germany before the rise of Hitler. The failure of scholars to debate serious matters which potentially affect public life might lead politicians to believe their policies are unimpeachable. The victory of Germany (Prussia) over France in the Franco-Prussian War led scholars to adopt an ideology of imperialism uncritically and to believe that greater territorial gains could be made with improved technology and military preparedness. This idea was implemented in World War 1. By 1933 many academics had moved enthusiastically from the openness of analysis over to the emerging political view of the worship of science and racial superiority. Edward Shils, a biographer of Weber, notes: "Nevertheless the capitulation of so many German academic figures to the Nazi regime may be plausibly interpreted as evidence of the correctness of Max Weber's diagnosis regarding the complaisance of the German academic profession in its eager subservience to the authority of the state and the erosion of its moral rectitude."[6]

A number of writers have participated in the attack on the melting pot. It cannot be discerned from their writings whether they were fully aware of the consequences of their roles in this general and overall attack. But since about the 1920s, the direction of assimilation has changed; the melting pot theory and program have given way to cultural pluralism. At the turn of the century the melting pot philosophy was the dominant one, and Americans thought, in general, that the country was large enough to absorb and remold divergent individuals who entered. Israel Zangwill epitomized this idea in his well-received play, around 1904, entitled *The Melting Pot.* It was the hope of America; the only way to bring millions of people with different backgrounds, life-styles, and values into a homogeneous group able to live peaceably with each other no matter what their histories. All were potentially of the American stripe.

Did the melting pot ideal decline because it was pragmatically un-workable, or was there a fundamental change in the tolerance of Americans toward separate cultures which were supposedly unequal? Certainly, as more groups learned about themselves, they found they were not wholly without merit as they had sometimes been told.[7] Maybe some groups, in a phase of cultural revival, were temporarily diverted from the basic ideal of the melting pot. The instance of black America's rediscovery of and identification with Africa may be a case in point. The third generation Japanese, Sansei, who seek to retain Japanese values, may be another. Descendants of the original Americans, the Indians, see much that is beautiful in their culture and are not keen about being submerged in modern technical society.

Are these temporary movements, understandable within the context of the times when people have become partially liberated from the mental hold a technically more advanced culture has maintained over them? Breaking the colonial and psychological bonds can be a liberating experience for many, but eventually all must return to the fundamental problem. Can there be an America characterized by cultures basically different yet within the mainstream of American life?

Brewton Berry notes that after World War 1 millions of immigrants could not speak, read, or write English. Less than half the foreign-born white males of voting age were citizens. Thousands of organizations flourished among the foreigners, including newspapers and periodicals published in foreign languages. Immigrants were concentrated in "colonies" in the cities. Under these conditions, the Americanization movement was born. Deliberate, organized efforts were undertaken to divest the immigrant of his foreign heritage; to teach him English and to make him a naturalized citizen with loyalty to American institutions.[8]

Berry feels this movement was based on a misconception of the process of assimilation. It ignored the values of the culture of the immigrants, which, it was assumed, they would discard as old garments. It implied that American culture was a finished product; that Anglo-Saxon culture was superior. The movement suggested a spirit of coercion, condescension, and suppression. It was resented and defeated by those at whom it was directed.

Berry accounts for the demise of the Americanization movement by the actions of immigrants themselves, not by the rejection of immigrants by the general American population. But there is little evidence that immigrants in general preferred to retain their old ties, though some no doubt did. The record shows that with or without help the white immigrants managed, for the most part, to become part of dominant America. The choice of any subject people to remain outside the mainstream or to join it was not left with them but was determined by outside forces. All would have joined the mainstream if they could. The general tenor of the times promoted the integration and assimilation of immigrants who did not wish to have their lives stigmatized for receiving special help. If the immigrants became acceptable to the American public, it was not because of some inherent trait or quality but because of the desire of the Americans to incorporate them into their society.

It is less disturbing that the melting pot did not happen than that the ideal was abandoned by the American people. Simpson and Yinger indicate:

During World War 1 many people were made aware of the problem of minorities by the discovery here, in times of crisis, of partially assimilated national groups. They were shocked at the failure of the "melting pot" idea. Antiforeignism increased, immigration restrictions were tightened and some started to wonder whether the melting pot idea might itself be adequate.[9]

Nativists opposed to the melting pot objected to immigration from the time of the American Revolution. Some academics have always been on their side. But there was little respected theoretical support for this position until it was given academic credence by Nathan Glazer and D. P. Moynihan. They tried to define an American as follows:

In any case, the word "American" was an unambiguous reference to nationality only when it was applied to a relatively homogeneous social body consisting of immigrants from the British Isles, with relatively small numbers from nearby European countries. When the numbers of those not of British origin began to rise, the word "American" became a far more complicated thing. Legally, it meant a citizen. Socially, it lost its identifying power, and when you asked a man what he was (in the United States), "American" was not the answer you were looking for. In the United States it became a slogan, a political gesture, sometimes an evasion, but not a matter-of-course, concrete social description of a person.[10]

Glazer and Moynihan continue to give solace to the pluralistic position by attributing characteristics to ethnic groups which they may not completely deserve. They state: "The ethnic groups of New York are also interest groups."[11] The implication seems to be that people of different ethnicities may not have the same or similar interests. But schoolteachers, for instance, have the same interests in getting better salaries and working conditions, regardless of national origin or ancestry. Would Glazer and Moynihan call them an ethnic group? The same may be said of automobile and dock workers, policemen, and myriad occupational specialists. Glazer and Moynihan assert: "The ethnic group is something of an extended family or tribe."[12] By locating the feeling of a group within the depths of its origin, the family or tribe being the most ancient of groups, Glazer and Moynihan imply that such feelings are natural and inescapable. Yet they also state:

The American descendants of immigrants diverge markedly from the people of the old country. American descendants of Germans seem no more committed to the unity of Germany and the defense of Berlin than other Americans. The foreign policy of the American-Irish seems to have nothing in common any more with the foreign policy of a neutral Eire, and the political outlook and culture of Americans of Italian descent seem to have little in common with what one can see in Italy. . . . The powerful assimilatory influences of American society operate on all who come into it, making the children of immigrants and even immigrants themselves a very different people from those they left behind.[13]

If ethnicity were important, the foundation of ethnicity being the country or region from which the immigrants came, it would seem that there would continue to be ethnic allegiance to the country of one's origin. As quickly as ethnics became successful in America, they would return to their old countries where they could be with their fellow ethnics. But this seldom happens. They all give up ethnicity as soon as they can.

A general stratagem of the academic who opposes the melting pot is to show that it has not worked in other cultures. Berry argues that Rumanians, Germans, and Magyars could not get along in the Transylvanian plateau in central Europe, though they had lived in fairly close contact for nearly one thousand years. Religion was a dividing factor, with Calvinism, Roman Catholicism, Unitarianism, Greek Catholicism, and Greek Oriental faiths providing the axes of conflict. Food and dress preferences of any one group became nasty habits in the eyes of others.[14] In Guatemala, the organization of the country into municipos, each one distinct with corresponding cultural differences, retards assimilation. In India there is conflict between the pastoral Todas, the agriculturalist Badagas, the artisan and musician Kotas, and the Kurumbas, who are sorcerers, food-gatherers, and dwell in the jungle. Although each of the cultural groups performs specific functions for the other, they have little in common.

After showing that the various groups cannot get along except in a very formalized and stratified situation, Berry implies that such must be the case in America. But a major difference between such groups as those mentioned and the American ethnics is that none of the other groups was impinged upon by an official ideology and mandate to form a single culture out of many. There was little conflict within these preliterate or precapitalistic cultures. But once they moved into the capitalist or modern orbit and recognized the weaknesses of their relative positions, they would not remain content with the usual social arrangements. The harijans (outcasts) of India, after becoming embroiled in the modern political economy, could no longer opt for separate and pluralistic status even though their lifestyle might be destroyed in the change.

From the period of about 1700 to about 1860, the problem of what to do with newcomers was not at issue. They were either inducted into indentured servitude or slavery, or they struck out for the slums of the emerging cities or the open spaces of the western frontier. Scholarship was nearly at a standstill, and academic analyses of the newcomer and alien people problem were handled at a religious, political, or generally emotional level. In fact, anyone whom the community did not like was simply asked to leave the area, which they frequently did, taking up with Indians or escaped slaves on the frontier. As long as there was somewhere to send people, it was not necessary to come to grips with the question of unwanted Americans.

When options ran out, beginning after the Civil War, America had to consider what was going to be said and done with her numerous new-comers. Assimilation, amalgamation, or cultural pluralism were possi-bilities, but they were not the only ones. The choices of expulsion, extermination, or the creation of a permanent lower class or caste were entertained, though these never gained any significant political support. Expulsion was the theory entertained in the case of blacks by some politicians such as Abraham Lincoln before the Civil War. He wanted to find them a home in Central America or send them all back to Africa.[15]

If a theory is to become widely accepted, it requires approval from some segment of society which acts in the role of legitimator. Over the period of human history various groups have played this role. In antiquity legitimation was based largely on brute force. The group with the greatest power could impose its will upon others with lesser power.

After a while the force of power gave way to the supposedly divine legitimacy of rulership, whether inherited or elected. Under this form of legitimacy the ruler required obedience of all subjects under his jurisdiction. Loyalty was unquestioned, and lives were imperiled for acts of disobedience to the dictates of royalty.

Still later, when the state emerged as a political entity, it assumed control of the loyalties of people, claiming obedience of all under its power. The state established laws by which to govern the lives of its subjects. Now an act was legitimate if it met the requirements of the law. Yet law has been vague and unclear in many cases. As states became larger, with laws representing competitive preserves of privilege, law started to lose out as the ultimate legitimator.

In a large society experts function in every field. The expert has a substantial amount of knowledge or skill in a limited area and is believed able to deal with problems in his field outside the knowledge of the common man. Extensive study, completion of curricula, experience, and successful independent productivity in a field are some general criteria establishing expertise. Once expertise is established, that status can be used to impress or legitimate. The mass media use experts to certify the quality of products so that more may be sold. Industry uses experts to iron out problems in all areas of production, management, staff relations, and marketing.

Many experts have gained their knowledge as members of college faculties where they concentrate intensely on special problems in their research or analyses. The number of experts found among the academic ranks is very large. Indeed, they constitute a source of instant expertise. A widely-received book written on a subject might establish a professor as an expert on that topic. It usually suggests or claims that he has done a certain amount of reading, thinking, and research and has insights into the problem which laymen do not have.

As Dr. Fruchtbaum suggests, some professors combine ideology with expertise, and often the two cannot easily be separated.[16] The expertise of the professor can hardly be separated from his ideology, though he might make a few opening statements in his report naming his biases or trying to placate his audience and keep them under control. In the social sciences, says Fruchtbaum, ideology and expertise are so intimately bound up that they can be disentangled only with great intellectual difficulty, if at all.

But how does this relate to pluralism? The pluralist adherent attempts to win over the public by showing that some famous person in the past or present believes in the strategy. In Seymour W. Itzkoff's *Cultural Pluralism and American Education*, John Dewey is given credit for believing strongly in pluralism. Dewey, born in a small New England town in 1895, became a professor in the Midwest, first at the University of Michigan, then Minnesota, then Chicago. He later moved to Columbia University. Dewey never believed in the city and equated it with anonymity caused by industrial society. The machine dominated the lives of men. Men, because of the nature of their work, had little responsibility to their communities. They lived in apartments and tenement houses and knew few of their neighbors. The urban person was anonymous, alienated, and undeveloped. Dewey yearned for the security of the small town where face-to-face relations predominated. He thought the smaller communities within which traditional religious and economic beliefs were rooted could be a guide for the social structure of America where democracy should serve human needs.

Dewey's pluralism rested on the idea that the family structure of the intradependent community of the small town or village could be preserved in the cities. He did not suggest that the small town would breed the liberal values needed to operate in the larger society. Small towns in the Midwest and North have generally been homogeneous by race but pluralistic by religion and social class.[17] Antagonisms based on the latter two factors have been every bit as problematic as those based on race.

Immigrants since the 1880s (the New Immigration) understood, more clearly than those of the Old Immigration (persons from northern and western Europe) that America is fundamentally a hybrid culture. The Civil War and its aftermath, for quite some years, blunted the enthusiasm of Americans to include persons of non-English background in its population unless those persons were willing to settle for second class citizenship. The credibility of the idea of tolerance was weakened by the mistreatment of black Americans in the South and the urban slums. New immigrants were less willing to compete for equality, since they were arriving from European ghettos which, even at their best, were considerably less promising than the opportunities offered even in the encapsulated enclaves in America where they were forced to congregate.

Immigrants naturally fell back on their ethnic separateness, attempting to build or revive institutions which would take them out of conflict with the whites, at least on a temporary basis. Direct challenges to Anglo hegemony had to be postponed by the New Immigrants until they could gain a secure place from which to mount an attack for first class citizenship. Parallel institutions such as ethnic schools and churches were interpreted by some observers as evidence of the desire of the immigrants to retain their separate institutional structures. Between the 1870s and the 1920s ethnic groups elaborated their largest and most noticeable institutional structures; their development corresponded to the period when America was most hostile as a place to live. The delayed reactions of many diehard Confederate sympathizers (and this group included important northerners) kept the movement toward civil rights from gaining momentum until around the beginning of World War 2. Immigrants were forced to remain in their ghettos because of a general leaning toward racism throughout the country. The longer they remained in their slums, the greater the tendency for them to justify their placement in theoretical terms. Soon it became fashionable to emphasize their nationality in front of the hyphen before "American."

The climate in which immigrants could demand first class citizenship could not arise unless the blacks pressed their case. During the long period from the 1870s through the 1920s, nearly all immigrant groups had adjusted to manual labor, poverty, and second class citizenship. The slums contained a disproportionately large number of poor immigrants, the prisons and jails were filled with immigrants from eastern and southern Europe, and the factories were manned by immigrants whose English was not good. Education of immigrants fell far below national expectations. Yet they still did not press for citizenship. During that period mainly black Americans, with the help of some liberal whites, continued the fight for America to honor its pledge to provide equality for its citizens. Immigrant groups, through a combined application of their own logic and fear, allowed the erosion of the civil rights of all non-English Americans. Their justification of their own ghettos was understandable in the presence of such works as Madison Grant's *The Passing of the Great Race* written in 1916. Dr. Berkson argued against equality for all by suggesting separate communities for different ethnic groups. He was mainly concerned with Jews from the "unassimilable" cultures of eastern Europe who migrated to America, but his logic might apply to other groups as well.[18] Later Henry Pratt Fairchild's *The Melting Pot Mistake* argued that immigrants could make but a poor contribution to America because their genes and experiences were inferior.

Prominent professors in American social science today legitimate certain programs which are to be implemented in this country or abroad. They conduct important studies and present available information in such a way as to suggest that a particular course of action is logical and reasonable. With respect to ethnic policies, some professors have gained quite significant places as legitimators. With the demise of the melting pot philosophy, professors present data which show that pluralism is the most feasible or acceptable of the various theories. And, of course, once the data are elaborated, the theory can be made to agree with it. In other words, since powerful leaders hope that the melting pot will fail, support is being built up by use of academic legitimators for the pluralistic strategy. (It is not suggested that professors planned the demise of the melting pot philosophy. Its destruction was probably engineered by forces much higher in policymaking positions.) A few examples from the writings of well-known social scientists on the question of ethnic assimilation will illustrate this function of academics. A 1974 book entitled *Cultural Pluralism,* edited by Edgar G. Epps, provides a convenient basis for analysis. It contains writings by prominent social scientists.

Thomas Pettigrew's observations are often the basis of governmental policy. He states: "The long-term goal is not complete obliteration of cultural pluralism, or distinctive Negro areas, but rather the transformation of these ghettos from racial prisons to ethnic areas freely chosen or not chosen."[19]

Pettigrew, of course, knows that in America an ethnic area is never formed by choice. It is an imposition, evidence of restriction of movement, of the lack of opportunity for upward mobility within the general society. An ethnic area in a supposedly or ideally nonethnic country like America is a pathology. Even the gilded ghettos of affluence are fabrications. By chance alone, given a normal distribution of ethnic and class groups, there would be no concentration of people living together with any ascribed characteristics in what are considered ethnic areas. If an area is ethnic, it represents the work of factors keeping other people out or hemming the residents in, more than it does some desire on the part of those to live together to the exclusion of other people. Pettigrew further states: "Yet a policy concentrating exclusively on integration, like one concentrating exclusively on enrichment, runs its own danger of worsening the situation. As many black spokesmen correctly point out, a single-minded pursuit of integration is likely to blind us to the urgent requirements of today's black ghettos."

Pettigrew's attempt to straddle the fence and placate all sides is evident. Integration would be a step toward the dissolution of the black ghetto, something which should have high priority in the politics of social change. Pettigrew knows well that the ghetto is pathological and the sooner it is dissolved the better, and the sooner blacks of the ghetto can be absorbed into the middle class.[20]

Andrew Kopan's position is similar to that of Pettigrew when he states: "Hence, the melting pot, so gloriously expounded by Crèvecoeur two centuries ago and praised by Zangwill's characters some sixty years ago, is in reality a myth. The melting pot, as we have seen, simply failed to melt."[21] He goes on to say, supporting the cultural pluralism hypothesis: "Cultural pluralism has given America its strength. Immigration has made the United States a world power of over 200 million people. . . . As its motto—*E pluribus unum*—proclaims, the United States remains truly one nation out of many people."

Kopan seems quite confused. He incorrectly identifies the melting pot as a myth when he might have used the term ideal. That melting has not taken place is not because of its impossibility but because of calculated efforts aimed at revising the American dream of the equality of mankind. The people have melted but the class structure has not. Preoccupation with complexion by people like Kopan distracts from the promise and reality of the melting pot. Of the 225 million odd Americans probably no more than 10 percent could be classified as racially pure.[22] The class system operates in a mechanical way to distribute people into so many gradations as to render the behavior of any individual unpredictable regardless of his ethnicity. In other words, ethnicity has lost its meaning, but class has not. If there are serious restrictions on people today, it is because of their poverty and not because of their ethnicity.[23]

Kopan's claim that America is one nation of many people is more an argument in support of the melting pot hypothesis than of cultural pluralism. America is probably the only country in the world where significant melting has occurred, blurring both ethnic and social class lines. In Latin America race has been melted but class is stronger than ever. In America race and class are disappearing at about the same speed. There are no longer "many people" of America, there are one people, some of whom carry on a few cultural practices of their ancestors. There are very few truly ethnic Americans left. Not even groups like the Mormons, Amish, Mennonites, and Hutterites are outside the American tradition; they cannot be viewed as truly distinct groups. The number of Indians living on reservations is smaller than the number living off. Even reservation Indians do not always live in traditional ways. Governmental projects, managed by the Bureau of Indian Affairs, are usually aimed at bringing Indians into more modern standards of living. The remaining ethnic people are remnants of the lowest class strata of the old cultures of which they were original members. Those who insist on acting ethnic are really "pop" or "academic" ethnics capitalizing on their ethnicity for monetary, psychological, or other gains. Even the most recent immigrants, the Southeast Asians and those from the Caribbean, have been unable to establish genuine ethnic communities. America simply is not fertile soil for the establishment of ethnic communities, and it is continuously finding ways to eradicate those managing to persist.

Kopan leads us astray when he states that America's strength derives from the differences inherent in her essentially immigrant population. If strength resided in ethnic differences, then countries in Africa, South America, and Europe would be strong. They have had dozens of competing ethnic groups for centuries and today they are mostly examples of weakness and poverty, not strength. Social differences are divisive, for they promote social stratification. They are not strength-producing, as Kopan wrongly reasons. South Africa understands very clearly that perpetuating differences within promotes weakness. This is why she has imposed the concept of external Bantustans, or separate development of indigenous Africans, while appealing to the unity of whiteness among the Europeans of that country.

Alfredo Castaneda writes: ". . . the cultural pluralists' position will be redefined in order to show the value of democratic cultural pluralism and biculturalism in education."[24] He opts clearly for pluralism as a form of adjustment of Mexican-Americans to American life.

Reed Ueda notes that Japanese-Americans have adopted a role to prove to themselves and to white Americans that they are the most

American of the ethnics. The cost to them is heavy psychologically, for they remain half-men, always acting. They do not wish to do anything which would upset the drama, to alter the image they have sought to cultivate among themselves and American whites. For the Japanese-Americans pluralism is a strategy to gain entry into the white middle class. They behave and achieve according to standards set by that class, something unmatched by few groups in or out of that class.[25]

Barbara Sizemore, an experienced educator and observer of the black problem, falls victim to the mystique of cultural pluralism. She feels that cultural and ethnic groups struggle to control the institutions which define their existence. A school based on an aggregate model rather than one of specialization will promote cultural pluralism. Such pluralism will be founded on equality of power. Yet Professor Sizemore uses as her example of power a Chicago organization called Woodlawn Experimental School District Program, funded by the federal government in one of the ten poorest of the seventy-five city community areas. Although the experiment in community organization for self-help was laudable, the local unit did not have the power the professor envisaged. The Chicago Board of Education maintained veto powers over Woodlawn.[26]

Judson Hixon adds to the reasoning for pluralism by suggesting:

Black concepts and values are not manifested in dominant institutions. Thus, those who display competence and power, especially the power to define social reality, become, for better or worse, sources of legitimation. It is this power that blacks are striving for in their demands for community-relevant and community-controlled schools. If blacks cannot make their values a major part of the dominant culture, they can at least control the legitimation process in the educational institutions that so profoundly affect the children in their charge.[27]

Edward J. Barnes, in summarizing his observations on minority group education, says: "A critical strategy necessary to break the familiar cycle of [underachievement] involves an explicit recognition of the child's community, group, and culture."[28] Barnes is arguing directly for pluralism under the guise of the equality of black and white culture.

Edgar Epps, in closing *Cultural Pluralism*, notes that most of the contributors believe racism is implicit in the melting pot philosophy, and that they stress values of respect for diversity in cultural pluralism. Epps says the typical school with a melting pot program requires that minority children regard their own culture as inferior and abandon it. He feels that the assimilationist view is a reformist position which looks to such strategies as integration, reorganization of school financing, curriculum revision, and compensatory education to eradicate inequities in the system. Such reforms, if successful, would, according to Epps, eliminate race and ethnicity as discriminatory factors, but leave intact these aspects of the educational system which discriminate according to social class. Since nonwhite families are more likely than white families to be found in the lower class, such reforms would not likely eliminate group differences in social position.[29]

Professor Epps does not tell us that there will be no class system among blacks if there is cultural pluralism or separatism. Those at the bottom of the social ladder are unlikely to feel better, no matter who keeps them there. A black master is no better than a white one, as rioting in South Africa's Soweto ghetto shows. The 1976 riots were directed at black storekeepers and other persons with vested interest in the perpetuation of racial separation in that country. Epps concludes:

To improve minority education there is a need for improved curricula, better teaching, and a more equitable allocation of resources. There is also need for a strong commitment to the goals of cultural pluralism. The community and the school should work together to achieve these common goals, and schools must be more responsive to diversity in American society. If the educational system fails to respond to the needs of oppressed groups, it will continue to promote the development of a rigidly stratified, racially segregated society.

All writers in this volume were in favor of cultural pluralism. Whether they were picked for their partiality we do not know. With so many people from the great schools and think tanks of the country saying the same thing, legitimation is given to the idea of cultural pluralism as being right in itself and as what the people want.

In 1977 Melvin Tumin and Walter Plotch edited a book entitled *Pluralism in a Democratic Society.* It is a collection of papers presented by established ethnicists at a B'nai B'rith conference sponsored by the U.S. HEW's Ethnic Heritage Center. Conferees duly made their cases for pluralism, as their consultantships required them to do. There was not one dissenter in the group, although there is substantial dissent regarding the whole issue of ethnic and cultural pluralism as it applies to America.[30]

James P. Comer became disenchanted with the melting pot in the 1960s. He, like many other black scholars, felt that a new rationale was needed to explain the failure of blacks to become fully integrated into the American system.

The *melting pot* myth has obscured the critical role of group power in the adjustment of white immigrant groups in this century. When immigrants were faced with discrimination, exploitation, and abuse, they turned in on themselves. Sustained psychologically by the bonds of their cultural heritage, they maintained family, religious, and social institutions that had great stabilizing force. The institutions in turn fostered group unity.[31]

Comer's analysis of the strength of immigrant institutions as a model which might be emulated by black Americans faced with problems similar to those immigrants faced one hundred years ago is not convincing. If immigrants turned in on themselves, sustaining themselves psychologically by their cultural heritage, there is no reason why they should not have continued sustaining themselves in this way once they became a part of the American mainstream. Indeed, logic would suggest that if this was working positively for the immigrants, they would not willingly have given it up. The truth is that as long as immigrants remained "turned in on themselves," strongly engrossed in their own culture, they cut themselves off from the strength of the greater culture, and added to or maintained their status as second class citizens. The immigrant experience shows that there are no groups which persisted in cultural habits sharply divergent from American ones and still received all rights of citizenship. Immigrants prospered, not through withdrawal into the immigrant subculture but through involvement in the major culture, even when this necessitated breaking away from the immigrant culture. The majority of immigrants made the decision to renounce their Old World ties, devaluing their Old World heritage, and opt for the more open opportunities, but lesser psychological security, of the general American society.

No group adhering to its old ways has been able to progress far to take advantage of as much as America has to offer. Japanese who keep their old ways of doing things remain Japanese, not Americans. Poles who continue to speak only Polish cannot hope for all they might achieve, because they are restricted by culture and handicapped in their effort to achieve social mobility. No Pole can hope to remain within the security of Little Poland in Chicago and experience the opportunities and achievements of first class citizenship.

Black Americans, though lately becoming more verbally aware of their culture, must obey the same logic as other groups formerly excluded from the mainstream. They are learning that America means an absence of ethnicity; that the very concept of ethnicity is incompatible with the philosophy of the country. In order to become 100 percent American one must give up allegiance to his ethnic group, for ethnicity is not important in a country where the population is basically ethnic and immigrant. In America ethnicity is nothing special.

2

THEORIES AND PLURALISM

Theories of cultural pluralism operate under various names. One of the most common is the conflict model of social science. Conflict theorists attempt first to discredit the equilibrium, homeostasis model, which is based on social harmony, peace, and brotherhood. They show that functional theory supports the status quo,[1] and appeal to the ideas of leading social scientists who have adopted the conflict theory in their work. A good example of this style of work is seen in an article by Lewis Killian and Charles Grigg, entitled "Racial Crisis in America: Leadership in Conflict."[2] They note that American sociologists and psychologists had adopted, by the mid-twentieth century, a utopian model of social adjustment, harmony, and absence of prejudice as an ideal. There was no conflict model in the social sciences. Even Gunnar Myrdal's idea of American race relations was basically a utopian concept where the American ideal—equality—would finally control the lives of men.[3]

Killian and Grigg argue that the theme of conflict as a basic social process has been present in sociology from the time of L. F. Ward, Albion Small, R. E. Park, and Charles Cooley. Each of these men played significant roles in the development of American sociology, from its founding in the mid-1800s into the first third or so of the twentieth century. Present adherents to the conflict theme are such scholars as Ralf Darendorf, Lewis Coser, and Ernest Borinski.

Joseph Himes, a black sociologist, obviously is impressed with the conflict hypothesis and argues that racial conflict has several beneficial consequences. According to Himes, conflict changes structural relations, leading toward black equality with whites, whereas old relations assumed fixed positions of superiority and inferiority. Racial conflict serves to solidify blacks and whites around core values respected and sought by both groups, thus producing greater unity in the society. Identity of each group is enhanced by and through the process of conflict with another racial group.[4]

Killian and Grigg, Borinski, and Joseph Himes are all writing from a perspective in a time during which conflict was most pronounced. They correctly observe that conflict was always a fundamental aspect of American race relations but fail to note that conflict might not have occurred if relations had been equal in America. It is hazardous to infer that a process is basic because it has been going on for a long time, when the conditions generating the conflict have not changed greatly. If these writers are saying that society cannot have social security, and thus absence of conflict for scarce goods and status, they should show some data that this is a rational conclusion. Much conflict is found in Western society because of its very heterogeneity and inequalities under a single set of norms. It is doubtful that proportionately as much conflict is found within preliterate Eskimo, Bushman or even more modern societies where wealth and status are more equally distributed. The proportion of conflict that is found in West Germany, England, or America, where the predominant orientations are capitalistic, does not exist in the Scandinavian countries. Small, culturally homogeneous societies, such as the Hutterites and Amish, strive to mitigate conflict and are relatively successful in doing so. If conflict were a basic process, it would be difficult to circumvent. But the American military forces, for instance, do not have a great deal of internal conflict because those societies are rationally planned for efficiency and social harmony.

As blacks made gains toward equal rights, some say through the method of conflict, other minority groups began to adopt their methods. American Indians, perhaps the most depressed people in North America, began to complain about their second class citizenship. In order to show that they had legitimate grievances, they tried to show first that they were a distinct people with a distinct culture. It was embarrassing to Indians to lag in terms of equal rights when they were classified as whites by laws passed to exclude blacks. In some cases, however, (interracial marriage, for instance) Indians are classified as blacks.[5]

In 1969 Vine Deloria, Jr. published a book entitled *Custer Died for Your Sins* in which he discussed the "white man's problem," defining it as a situation in which one saw blacks as draft animals, Indians as wild animals, Orientals as domestic animals, and Mexicans as humorous lazy animals. Civil rights laws have made these categories of minorities merely ex-blacks, ex-Indians or whatever they were at first; white attitudes toward them have not changed fundamentally. Deloria's analysis is a pluralistic one; he believes "whites are after Indian lands and resources." He also believes there will remain the question of the legal relationship of the Indian tribes to the federal government. Indians are the true owners of the land and others are merely usurpers. Deloria likewise believes civil rights laws make little difference because the "basic thrust is to keep the black out of society and harmless. . . . It is foolish for a black to depend upon a law to make acceptance of him by the white possible."[6]

Deloria fantasizes: "Historically, each group has its own road to travel. All roads lead to personal and group affirmation. But the obstacles faced by each group are different and call for different solutions and techniques. . . ." He feels that Indians have been able to deal directly with the federal government because they had a recognized status within the constitutional framework. Indian people have the option of total withdrawal from American society because of their special legal status. Blacks, likewise, he suggests, must have a homeland where they can withdraw, drop the facade of integration, and be themselves.

Deloria faces a few critical problems in taking his pluralistic stance. He obviously believes that groups may live together, interacting without sharing culture, problems, and concerns. His main point is that Indians are a separate people, but he does not seem to understand that they did not, and do not, define themselves. More powerful social systems defined them first, without their significant input, and while the power is still unequally distributed they still cannot participate in the definitional process. Yet Indians may no more withdraw from society than blacks. As any Indian historian will verify, even the reservation lands of Indians have not been enough to shield them from the problems and concerns of the larger society. The legal status of the Indian can be traded, changed, and rechanged, at the whim of government so long as he remains tied to the reservation ghetto.

There is scant evidence that any large group can separate itself from the general American society. The larger the group, the greater the number of ties it has to the larger society. It is through these ties that the solidarity of the group is broken down. When a large number of persons are tied into a large number of bureaucracies and agencies on the basis of first class citizenship, their old cultural groups weaken considerably. Deloria's dilemma is serious. He must trade first class citizenship for the imagined security of the reservation ghetto. Even reservation Indians are finding this a hard choice to make. In fact, so many Indians are disappearing into the mainstream that the federal government has had to increase its program of granting aid to Indians if they can show they qualify for inclusion on the Indian roll and therefore for protected status.

Deloria is being used as a member of an ethnic group to legitimate or approve cultural pluralism so as to make it more acceptable to other minority groups. But he is not convincing when he suggests that blacks give up the goal of integration, which means giving up the drive for first class citizenship, to press for their own homeland. Blacks already have a homeland, like the Indians, which no one wants to share, not even their own members—the slums and ghettos where they have been forced to live. The pluralistic position encourages blacks to be happy with the slums and work hard to develop them. The record shows, however, that more and more blacks are leaving the slums.[7] This trend indicates that there is no ideological commitment to the slums even though commitment would be necessary for a group endorsing the pluralistic position.

What happened to the melting pot idea? Have scholars been bought off to give legitimacy to the idea that it will not work? Are there no examples of it working? Obviously ethnic and cultural pluralism could not work in the military forces. There everything is done to melt men and women into an efficient fighting force. Ethnicity is recognized as little as possible, the tendencies to allow blacks to use the black power salute and afro haircuts notwithstanding. In homes for the aged pluralism is not practiced to any significant degree. Concentration is on adjustment to aging.

But we must ask a more difficult question. Is there a plan afoot to change the American people from the idea of a single culture, one in which all groups are blended, giving up distinctive traits of Old World or indigenous separate cultures?

3

THE RISE OF THE ETHNIC MANIPULATORS

The manipulation of the ethnic American is occuring along the same lines as the black American. As black living standards continued to rise, the result of war spending and self-assertion through the courts, blacks were discouraged from seeking equality with whites. The media showed they could achieve more and be happier as a separate group. Achievements by such persons as Booker T. Washington and Dr. George W. Carver of Tuskegee, Marian Anderson on the concert stage, Joe Louis in the boxing ring, Benjamin O. Davis, Sr., and his son in the military, and businessmen such as representatives of the North Carolina Mutual Insurance Company of Durham, were used to create racial pride in young blacks. By being proud of their race and striving mainly within a black orbit, they felt able to resist pressure from integratory efforts and to emphasize black community development.

There are plenty of grounds for achievement within the separate black community, and some encouragement was given for such achievement. Overlooked, however, was the fact that the black business and professional sectors could accommodate only a small portion of those blacks who wanted to succeed in areas outside of common labor. Black business could not grow sufficiently to allow employment of the increasing numbers of qualified young blacks from the colleges and the few professional schools designated as for blacks.[1] The vast majority of blacks were stranded in common labor, either in the towns or on the farms, and had hit the upper limits of achievement possibilities by the time they were in their mid-twenties. It was clear to nearly all that the future would not be bright for those who sought their fortunes wholly within the confines of the black community.

After the Korean War, and the *Brown* decision, other factors started to decrease the opportunities for achievement within the black community. The thrust toward equal opportunity outside enabled more blacks to seek and obtain employment beyond the traditional market for their skills. More opportunities were found outside the structure of the black community.

In general, black communities lost their schools and most of the payrolls associated with them following integration.[2] After a few years, the few blacks who were retained as teachers in white schools started to purchase homes in the white communities. Poverty programs were envisioned as a substitute for the loss of the business and professional class who were vacating the black ghettos. But uncertain fundings of these programs, occasioned by political manipulation, practically forced them out of business in the early 1970s. Urban renewal virtually wiped out the slums of hundreds of cities so that blacks remain as pockets of traditional slum dwellers only in some of the largest and most difficult to rehabilitate inner cities.

Prosperity and improved social outlook for first class citizenship muted the thrust toward black separatism in the general population. In many of the colleges, however, students continued to give verbal support to the separatist role and some bitterly turned their socialization away from the direction of whites and sought to enrich themselves wholly through black associations.

The few percentage points gained by blacks in relation to whites on the scale of prosperity over the last decade encouraged the ethnics to feel that blacks were gaining ground on them; with so much federal help blacks would soon catch up and surpass them in their living standards. Ethnic manipulators began saying white ethnics were being mistreated by the government in favor of the blacks and that to counter this development the ethnics should become militant. Gross appeals were made to the ethnicity of various groups which formerly had seen themselves as members of the white lower middle class and whose failure to rise into the middle class was due, apparently, to their private shortcomings. There were no significant and demonstrable structural limitations to the mobility of the white ethnic as there had been legal barriers to black mobility. Incredibly, the ethnic manipulators sought to show that white ethnicity could become a banner around which millions of "unmeltables" could rally in the way that black identity galvanized the blacks to bring about social change in the 1960s and early 1970s.

The history of America has shown a constant struggle to make the factor of background irrelevant in affecting or determining social outcomes. America has been the one place in the world where a man could say,

"To hell with background. It makes no difference that my parents or fore-parents were from Germany, Ireland, Africa, Russia, or elsewhere. It has no meaning and no consequence here." This has been a tremendous drawing card for America, really the only thing which differentiates it from the rest of the world. The concept of the irrelevance of background indicates that all may achieve equality and respect within a dynamic, productive, and free society.

But, ironically, at a time when the government is spending millions to bring about the eradication of background as a variable, some scholars are trying to convince people of the merit of their background in its most insidious form: race and ethnicity. Michael Novak, who recently discovered that he is Slovak, tries to convince his fellow ethnics there is something worthwhile in ethnicity.[3] He feels ethnic white Americans are looked down upon by others from some moral height. The poorest Alabama whites could think themselves superior to blacks and had the populist tradition to validate their patriotism and moral worth. But ethnic whites had no one to whom they could feel superior. In Chicago, and other cities, whites have vast insecurities about their own way of life. He pleads for them to be extended the same cross-cultural understanding extended to blacks. He asserts that the gains of black Americans were made at the expense of the white ethnics who have so very little to share with anybody. Novak contends that there are no rewards for integration, only penalties. When blacks move into the neighborhood everything begins to deteriorate. Intellectuals lose nothing by integration; the ethnics, everything. Novak asserts: ". . . ethnic memory is . . . a set of instincts, feelings, intimacies, expectations, patterns of emotions and behavior; a sense of reality; a set of stories for individuals—and for the people as a whole—to live out. . . . The ethnic group is one of the chief shapers of personal action and its significance."[4]

The principal theoreticians of the black separatist movement are white scholars who, upon reading a few books about the blacks' struggle for humanity, concoct plans for them. Charles Keil in *Urban Blues* tries to prove to blacks they have a distinctive culture to guard and protect. He thinks the African tradition, slavery, postslavery oppression, the re-emergence of the nonwhite world, and America's failure to allow integration, have combined to give the black a different reality, a different culture, and a unique perspective on American society that may be this nation's outstanding and redeeming virtue.[5]

While all may appreciate Keil's interest in black culture, few would agree that romanticizing the pathological aspects of the culture will convert them to strengths. The drunken bluesman moaning in the gutter; the money-grabbing charlatan preacher; the sadistic, castrating bitch of an old woman–the black matriarch; the hustler, and others are raised to a status of true perpetuators of black culture.

Keil evidently experiences a profound sense of guilt in his failure or inability to positively affect black life. He envisions the possibility of twisted white minds using genocide as the "final answer to the black problem." His reaction is a momentary romanticizing of black life which suggests that blacks should protect the weakest part of their existence: their cultural difference. Out of his fears he erects a program bound to confuse young blacks into believing they can escape the competition of modern society by taking flight into blackness. Keil perceives blacks as exotic and he probably experienced euphoria in understanding their culture.[6] But he has not offered a plan whereby blacks can get out of the ghetto and have access to the same chances and lifestyles that he takes for granted.

One strategy of opponents of the melting pot is to pin negative labels on those who believe in the assimilationist position. Lavender and Forsyth illustrate this point. They believe there is an assimilationist bias in American sociology. This bias has led to much analysis of the economic oppression of blacks and to little analysis of the status of minority non-blacks, who are more numerous than blacks: Indians, Catholics, and Jews, for instance. The authors suggest the assimilationist bias is "at least partly Marxist in origin."[7]

Lavender and Forsyth attempt to shore up their anti-melting pot position by linking assimilation with Marxism. They understand the impact of the word "Marxism" on general readers. They know they are frightened by the mention of the word and panic if any association is made of them with the Marxist position. They draw upon Andrew Greeley's statement that "the elites in American society have rediscovered ethnicity–hesitantly, fearfully, ambivalently."[8] Lavender and Forsyth are resorting to an old ploy they learned from their sociology of cultural diffusion. They think that if elites adopt a practice the rest of the population will do likewise. What these scholars forget is that elites created ethnicity and got the world in big trouble with it; remember slavery, the revolutionary and Civil wars, the Spanish American War, colonialism, the depression of the 1930s, Korea, the riots of the 1960s, Vietnam, and much else?

Analysis of each of the foregoing cases, and some others in the same categories which are unmentioned, would show that elitism generated great conflict, then relied upon ethnicity to become the connecting link between the elites and the rank and file, who the elites relied on for technical and military support. Ethnicity therefore becomes a tool with which to manipulate and control groups by convincing them that "the other people are really different from ourselves and are a threat to our way of life." There can be little disagreement with the idea that slavery and colonialism were slowed down wars, for they pitted groups, ideologically defined as different, against each other as a result of elitist logic and politics. A depression is a special kind of war. It is a conflict between those with the means of accumulating property and those trying to guard meager resources.

Slavery was an elitist response to the labor needs of colonial and postcolonial America. The ordinary citizen had no slaves and most could not acquire any. The slave was economically useful to the affluent slaveholder, but was a sharp wage competitor to those with no property or skill from which to derive status. The portions of America where slavery was not permitted were those in which yeoman farming and household stability through farm ownership could be achieved.

The revolutionary war was a consequence of colonial ideological divisions into intellectual groups, basically those for independence and those for continued colonial status. That a strike for independence should be taken was an intellectual and elitist decision, not one made by the rank and file of the colonists.

The Civil War occurred partly because of a schism created in the general population by intellectuals whose writings and influence sharpened the moral dilemma of slavery versus freedom. Abolitionist literature and action clashed sharply with that of the defenders of slavery. Lincoln captured the essence of the dilemma and intellectualized it into a technical problem when he suggested "the nation cannot survive half slave and half free."

Near the turn of the century, America entered a phase of colonialism. Elite and intellectual decisions merged to dictate the logic of the Spanish American War as they did to pave the way for the Great Depression of the 1930s. Even the Korean War was not based completely upon military contingencies. It was partially a consequence of an intellectual idea, at high levels, to contain communism in Asia. Vietnam followed the same logic.

The riots of the 1960s were not without intellectual bases. The decision of blacks to become violent resulted from ideological conflict between the accommodationism of Booker T. Washington, the withdrawal programs of Marcus Garvey and the Nation of Islam, the legalisms of the NAACP, the nonviolent counsel of Martin Luther King, Jr., and the angry rhetoric of black street intellectuals who could not envision change without bloodshed.

At a national level, the elite were the decision makers, as they have been in nearly every regime and time. The elite would have great difficulty functioning without significant intellectual underpinning. But clearly, people are going to be skeptical of anything the elite adopt for it will ultimately benefit the elite more than the general public. The elite of sociology will be unable to resurrect the myth of ethnicity, for all can see it is a fraudulent concept and practice. If anyone has lost credibility with the public, it is the elite, whether they are academic, political, or financial.

The connection between elitism and the manipulation of ethnic and racial groups was exposed by a few scholars, some of whom suffered loss of mobility for doing so. Lavender and Forsyth are most uncharitable to the late O. C. Cox, who vigorously rejected the pluralistic strategy.[9] Professor Cox was opposed to ethnic diversity. From the vantage point of his 73 years, 1901–1974, Cox understood clearly that in America ethnic diversity means conflict, hatred, and human exploitation. One reason he was not rebutted on this point was that scholars of vision and research saw merit in Cox's position. Parenthetically, Lavender and Forsyth fail to indicate that they have seen Cox's most famous work, *Caste, Class and Race,* or the other studies he made in his attempt to clarify the nature of race relations and its connection to capitalism.[10]

Since the emergence of the new ethnicity in the mid-to-late seventies the ethnic groups attempting to capitalize upon it have received little other than verbal encouragement from government officials. Talk of the strength of ethnicity has not been translated into publicly sponsored programs exclusively beneficial to any ethnic group qua ethnics. No Italian, Polish, Japanese, or other classes have been sponsored at the public school, college, or university levels purely as concessions to the new ethnic emphasis. There was agreement over the need for black studies, for all knew of black mistreatment, academic and real, and of the tangible benefits to be derived from blacks' discovery of themselves as positive individuals and people. It was less clear that most other groups had suffered similar handicaps. Fully assimilated persons of whatever ethnic background have not been encouraged through programs to resurrect their Old World values and lifeways. Even though considerable attention is being given to ethnicity at the university level, under the influence of the academic ethnics, it has yet to be implemented programatically, and all activities remain or continue in desegregatory postures. In spite of the clamorings of the ethnicists and pluralists, the schools, industry, universities, and major institutions remain guided by standards emphasizing unity rather than diversity. The federal government alone attempts to play the incompatible roles of encouraging ethnic separation and racial integration at the same time. It is quite doubtful that any fully assimilated American ethnics will be able to use the machinery of government to pull away from the mainstream by asserting their love for their Old World cultures.

Elitist manipulation of ethnicity has occurred at the national level, though not exclusively by governmental functionaries. Agencies and institutions with national visibility or influence may use ethnicity to further their own aims. Emphasis on ethnicity is a concession to pluralists who threaten to use their political strength to direct or alter courses of political, social, and/or economic action. It is alleged that under pluralism government will be more satisfactory. Ethnic emphasis placates sensitive groups which are disgruntled about their share of the resources. And these groups are rewarded in psychic capital. Elitists expect the ethnics to be satisfied with token appointees. They ask: How can the Slovaks complain if the secretary of state is one of them? What more do the Italians want? They've got the Mafia and the secretary of HEW. And the Chicanos? Isn't the secretary of the treasury Hispanic? Haven't we given several top positions to the blacks? Under the manipulatory strategy ethnic people are expected to be governed roughly according to the principles of "indirect rule."[11] The ethnic hierarchy will manage affairs of the group under the guidance of and for the enhancement of the elitist manipulators.

4

THE FALLACY OF CULTURAL PLURALISM

Sociologists argue over concepts, and much behavior study never gets beyond the definitional stage. They always ask for better and more accurate definitions or data. But definitions and data are already piled so high one can hardly get into the office of the typical sociologist. Emphasis on data collection and definitions serves to keep questions within the confines of the sociological vocabulary and prohibits their reaching a stage of utility in the wider society. Scholars can ask for more money to study the problems, which will produce additional definitions and data. The process is endless, and mankind remains mired in the same old problems. If a sociological solution is found, it is generally in favor of the ruling class. Nothing gets done for the lower classes, although some projects may appear to be so designed.

Within the sociological fraternity the same struggles are going on as within the general society. The structure provides an arena for men to compete for status, prestige, honor, and cash. People try to monopolize ideas in the discipline and do so through arrangements with book publishers who palm off books on unsuspecting students across the country. The more successful the book, the greater the prestige of the sociologist. Books are accorded prestige if sales are high. Thus, books as scientifically debatable as Arthur Jensen's essay on racial I.Q.s or as intellectually suspect as Nathan Glazer and Patrick Moynihan's *Beyond the Melting Pot* reflect the placement of the writers in the academic-economic marketplace and not the sound scholarship they are said to reveal. Even Gunnar Myrdal's *An American Dilemma* was suspect because he was so closely associated with ruling interests in America.

The great findings of social science are generally in support of the status quo—the ruling class. James Coleman's assessment of the futility of busing to achieve racial balance in the schools was a reinterpretation of his data and a change from his original position. One suspects Coleman may have been influenced by factors other than the data he purported to reanalyze. As a result of this orthodoxy, if a finding does not support the ruling class position, that finding is immediately declared suspect, radical, or revolutionary.

Presently, the pluralists are at pains to show the beauty and vitality of ethnic groups in order to convert millions to their elitist position. Current emphasis on ethnicity obscures the fact that the ethnic group is like a minority group—it is discriminated against. Where the general culture has been more interested in outsiders achieving citizenship, modern elitist manipulators encourage Old World persons to think of themselves as ethnic groups. By this logic they are expected to live in their own ghettos, as do the Poles in St. Louis, the poor Irish in Boston, and the Slovaks in Chicago. They may work in the larger culture but return nightly to their ghettos where they are told by master cultural sociologists, or their own scholars, that their way of life is highly desirable and superior to New World ways. They are not told that generations of second class status, first in the Old World, then in the New, have programmed them psychologically to accept their status. Noncompetitive persons find their status within their narrow ethnic groups but do not realize they are despised by mainstream peoples. The ethnics do not realize that this discrimination is keeping them in ghettos where job prospects are not much better than in black ghettos. When the group is white, they are encouraged to accept their discrimination by the application of the label "ethnic," so that they feel they are appreciated for their cultural uniqueness when this is in fact not the case. Attaching the label ethnic to a group, whether or not it is black, does not erase the fact that such a group is discriminated against.

Some scholars with little to lose, because they are already receiving all rights of citizenship, are prone to speak against the melting pot as a goal to be achieved by the minority population. An illustration of this position is seen in a book which appeared in 1970, entitled *Cracks in the Melting Pot*, by Melvin Steinfeld. In this work the author attempts to show that there had been a rejection of the myth of the melting pot by majority Americans and minority groups. In the second edition, in 1973, Steinfeld asserted that there are now fewer advocates of assimilation by coercion and that minority peoples are placing more emphasis on self-assertion, determination, and pride in the unique lifestyles of their cultural heritage. The author then went on to remind us that there are ethnic, class, and racial problems in just about every place in the world.

Some authors try to show that blacks who try to make race relations more harmonious are in reality misguided persons, confused by the rhetoric of assimilation and the melting pot. Data and evidence are scanty, but one would like to know what the payoffs are for scholars who advocate a departure from the melting pot ideal. Because a scholar becomes personally disenchanted with a process of social change, is he justified in making a case that such a process is not defensible for the minority group? In other words, why should a minority group member listen to a scholar's suggestions when they may not be any more impressive than their converse? What evidence is there that a separatist position makes more sense than a melting pot one? Even those scholars trying hardest to sell the goal of separation have not answered that question.

Social goals are not decided on the basis of scientific evidence alone. Values are always implied in their choice and attainment. It is when there is agreement on common values that problems can be reduced to their technical components. Thus the issues of separation, the melting pot, or some intermediate value such as cultural pluralism, must be defined first as values. Sometimes crises force sharp definitions of values. The revolutionary war was instrumental in clarifying the values of independence or colonial status of the Americans. A value is a concept. The allusion in the Pledge of Allegiance to "one nation" is a value, the attainment of which is a process of engineering. Values cannot be derived from scientific conclusions. Much in the social world rests upon value premises. The desirability of social goals which are in conflict cannot be resolved outside of the context of values.

White scholars are asking ethnics to renounce the melting pot philosophy without saying whether they would be willing to accord them respect under other arrangements. If they are philosophically opposed to the melting pot, they would not be willing to grant respect since they are aware that under separatism ethnics would not have first class citizenship. Is it possible that these scholars are looking for ways to remove the ethnics from their consciences by removing them from the interaction arena? They can do this by helping them to accept a separatist position.

Cultural pluralism is a bogus theory operating behind the mask of scientific and academic respectability. It emerges from those who represent the interests of the conservative establishment. The consequences of cultural pluralism for America are the same as for the countries of the developing world. In India and Africa, where nations are made of many cultural strains, separatism and irredentism have been carried to great extremes. Nearly every small group which feels its interests are not being protected wants to break away and form another sovereign country. Their situation is not very different from that of America two centuries ago. America's pluralism, insofar as it was a counter current to the ideal of cultural unity, led to little else but conflict. The colonists and Indians were pluralistic in that they represented two fundamentally different cultures. The Indians were practically wiped out and Anglo hegemony established. The Spanish and French tried to exist as separate groups, and their conflicts did not end until they were subdued militarily and a single culture was established. The remnants of subdued cultures are very shabby reminders of the vitality of those ways of life which fell by the wayside.

Before the period of the Civil War, the North and South claimed to represent two separate and equal ways of life, two cultures; and so America at that time was pluralistic. The bloodiest conflict the world had seen up to that time rent the nation. The culture of the South was destroyed, or at least weakened. Its major institution, slavery, was wiped out, and southern culture perpetuated mainly in myth and stereotype. Even after the Compromise of 1877 when federal troops were withdrawn from the South and segregation reinstituted, the culture of the South was rejected, even by the majority of southerners. It does not have a great deal of respect on a national scale even today.

As a political program, cultural pluralism capitalizes on the divisiveness of groups. It provides no practical way of allowing competing groups to reach equality. Pluralistic cultures clash over the unfair distribution of resources, which is inevitable so long as the we/they dichotomy of pluralism remains. Under pluralism force must be used to maintain equilibrium. The group with the greatest power at a particular time will command the resources. And since no group has a monopoly on science, politics, and technology, the balance of power can shift sharply within short spans of time, forcing the groups to concentrate resources on defense, which, at bottom, means aggression.

Russia and America represent the axes of a pluralistic world culture, communism and capitalism. International pluralism comes about through a balance of power, not a mutual respect by and for diverse cultures. These poles relate to each other through the threatened use of political and military power to enforce their positions.

Within the United States pluralism presents the same problem. Power is the principal ingredient in the pluralistic system. True, in a one-man, one-vote county, where blacks and whites are evenly divided, there may be a sharing of political offices. This was a technique often used during Reconstruction when blacks had legal rights and the franchise. Blacks, say, could have the sheriff's office if whites were given the office of tax collector. It may appear, therefore, that the two groups are respecting each other's culture when, in effect, the only thing that counts is power at the ballot box. As quickly as one or the other group achieves a numerical majority, power shifts in its direction. However, if one group obtains economic dominance in the form of, say, the establishment of a factory for which almost everyone in the area works, power drifts toward that group, nullifying the power generated by the numerical majority.

The underdeveloped nations of the world are characterized by cultural pluralism and incessant conflict. One-party states have emerged to melt the people into homogeneous working units, submerging their local ethnic and religious loyalties. In Africa, for instance, the concept of socialism, exemplified under such headings as "harambee," "Negritude," and "ujamaa,"[1] although justified in political terms, performs the same function philosophically as the concept "melting pot" in American life. In Africa conflict is referred to as tribalism. In America modern tribalism has been due to the presence of millions of immigrants who did not understand or appreciate American ways. Colonialists in Africa played upon tribalism to promote cultural pluralism while keeping power for themselves. In America those persons and institutions with vested economic interests in the preservation of divisiveness and conflict exploited American tribalism or ethnic pluralism to their advantage.

As the one-party state strives to mitigate the conflictive aspects of cultural pluralism in Africa and other developing countries, government will be forced to regulate such conflict in America. Government could become the equivalent of the one-party state. Groups perceiving themselves as different require special services to preserve their differences. Government becomes larger to make sure that groups are not overlooked and that they have legal recourse and redress. Governmental bureaucracy burgeons, and soon no group will have freedom because in the exercise of its freedom it would transgress the space and value of some other group. Pluralism allows members of conflicting ethnic groups to segregate each other in their minds. Categories are developed for the rival groups. No demand is made upon the mind of the segregator in behalf of the segregatee.

In caste-ridden India, for example, the outcasts' living conditions were scarcely viewed with alarm. Sleeping in streets, participating in many illegal activities, and experiencing the greatest hunger and deprivation were not outrageous to Indians of higher caste. They accepted these conditions as natural and bearing religious approval. America's own ethnic poor could likewise be overlooked and their unenviable living conditions attributed to their desire to retain their cultural uniqueness. Easy justification is offered for one group ignoring the other.

Pluralism for ethnics is also a form of yielding to paternalism. No ethnic subculture is strong enough to compete on equal terms with the general culture. For a while, during the 1960s, when the new self-awareness of blacks was such an electric force, some mistook this enthusiasm for cultural strength. The guilt of whites kept them from refuting the claim of black equality, and so they failed to point out to blacks that a restrictive culture which is not of the mainstream could not be competitive. Claiming respect for black culture gained respite for the whites. It bought a lull in time, breathing space for both parties, suspension of the struggle for a time. But it did not solve the problem. Dashiki-wearing, afro-headed blacks without the technical skills of the dominant society found themselves, in the majority of cases, headed for the unemployment offices.

The mystique of separatism soon ran its course. The 1960s black, then in his early teens or twenties, and justifiably impatient for change, seized upon nationalism as a tremendous tool. For a time, even through the early 1970s, he felt that through nationalism he would achieve anything he sought. The idea of remaking the world according to his requirements, which did not include whites, seemed feasible. He thought he could seize power and use the community to his advantage. He was wrong; misled. Today the hangover revolutionary is in his early or mid-thirties, and if he did not change his nationalistic, pluralistic orientation, he is today a bearded nationalist, angry, unemployed, or ineffective as he continues his rhetoric of rejecting middle class culture simply because it is white. He is totally out of character even in the black community, where some members have made enough progress through the open spaces in the system to cling precariously to a desirable standard of living.

There is no reason to believe that white ethnics would consolidate real gains as cultural separatists. Fortunately, assimilationist theory prevents America from going the way of the typical European country today impoverished by the hangovers of ethnic separation and cultural pluralism. Ireland is beset with the consequences of pluralism. Hundreds of years of stratification, based first on linguistics, then religious differences, then economics, have kept Ireland in the throes of revolution and violent social change. The Dutch, Flemish, and Walloons in Belgium have all tried to preserve their ethnic differences and have only succeeded in intensifying strife or settling into patterns of inequality which may have to be resolved by force. The Basques of Spain also cannot expect equality as long as they cling to the distinctiveness of their culture. Israel, new as nations go, shows every symptom of going the route of all other

Europe-based nations by trying to preserve ethnic differences largely by means of preserving differential positions and opportunities for the variety of ethnic and cultural groups of the land.

The black American, in the midst of a Europe-based society steeped in a history of hatred and dislike of other cultures, serves as a point around which the culture may unite. Black assimilation will probably be the solution to the majority of America's problems and, perhaps indirectly, for the rest of the European world. An assimilationist philosophy creates hopes as well as problems for the American people.

America's central problem is its treatment of its poor people, who are represented most clearly by the blacks. It is the one problem which confuses other cultures about America. Because of its failure to deal a hand of equality to the blacks, the world remains suspicious of America. In some places, like South Africa, the ill-treatment of millions of people is tied to America's treatment of its own minority peoples, especially the blacks. A decision by America to free its black hostages would revolutionize human relations in most of the world, for its example would exert a tremendous moral force upon the remaining countries with hostage peoples.

Assimilation portends one major problem, and that is its implementation. So much antiassimilationist rhetoric has been put forward that it would be difficult for some hard core obstructionists to close ranks around this value. Indeed, some might prefer to see America fail as an experiment in the social equality implicit in the assimilationist option.

For the white American assimilation of the black is a necessary step toward proving that Americans have broken away from the older European norms which recognized the importance of background. For the black American anything other than assimilationist melting pot ideology or practice will consign him to second class citizenship.

The fundamental difference between American and European politics (there are no significant differences in their cultures) is that America took the rather unusual step (a step founded in the Magna Carta) of providing for the preservation of individual liberties. These liberties were to be maintained even though one might be a member of a low status group. Categoric treatment of individuals because of social class or status factors would not be guaranteed. The real meaning of the Magna Carta was reiterated in the Bill of Rights of the Constitution and in the Civil War and later amendments prohibiting discrimination on the basis of age, race, and sex.

Eradication of categoric treatment of individuals based on race, age, or sex, left intact only opportunities to exclude on grounds of class.

But since many people are now in the money economy, large differences between individuals are being removed, though there are still major gaps between the wealthy and the poor.

5

DISABILITIES AND THE MELTING POT

Confusion regarding the concept of the melting pot derives partly from the way it is defined. Structurally, it requires the disappearance of a group into the dominant culture and the removal of all traces of the culture which has been melted. The implication is that unless the group disappears through social acceptance into the majority culture, melting has not taken place.

But preoccupation with definitional problems conceived in this way obscures another factor related to the melting pot process. Practically, an individual or group has melted into the major culture when disabilities are no longer suffered which are directly related to ascribed status. Another way of putting it is to ask: "What are the consequences of membership in a social category, whether it be ethnic, racial, or other? Does social membership affect one's ability to buy a house *if* he has the money?" Obviously it does not, for it is illegal to fail to sell to someone simply because of his race, faith, or values. "Is one denied the use of public facilities, the right to make contracts, the right to marry whomever agrees to be his or her spouse? Is one restricted to certain areas of town or to practice only certain professions or fields because of his race or ethnicity?" Clearly not. There is no category of behavior which all individual blacks or minority individuals suffer because of their membership in the group. If disabilities are not suffered as the result of placement in minority group status, can it be claimed that those persons are not assimilated into the dominant culture, the culture in which there is freedom?

Using the absence of disabilities as a criterion of assimilation creates some dilemmas for separatists. They must account for those ethnics who

47

are not discriminated against but who are participating in the dominant culture. They must also explain why certain members of the majority culture are not functioning in that culture with any degree of effectiveness. For instance, are poor whites any more assimilated into the dominant culture than upper income blacks?

That some minority members are not disabled means that they are assimilated into the dominant society. Thurgood Marshall, U.S. Supreme Court Justice, suffers no disability by virtue of his racial membership. Neither does Vice-Admiral Samuel Gravely, U.S. Third Fleet Commander, or William Coleman, former secretary of transportation, or Thomas Bradley, mayor of Los Angeles, or Clifton Wharton, former president of Michigan State University. What conceivable disabilities might Senator Edward Brooke suffer because of being black? Or Hank Aaron or Muhammad Ali or a thousand others? Not even the most bigoted or poorly placed white person could impose a handicap upon persons so placed in society. The number of ethnics who are not disabled is small compared to the total group, but their placement should argue for their assimilation, leaving the remainder on the disabled list. Each ethnic person who succeeds in shaking off disabilities should be added to the category of those who have melted into the general society.

Social science scholars have confused the meaning of assimilation with the *numbers* of minority group members constituting the lower socioeconomic class. Since lower class membership means exclusion from the main society, it should be clear that poor whites are not assimilated, though their proportions may be smaller than the proportion of blacks who are assimilated. Seen in this way, assimilation means absence of disabilities attributable to minority group membership. It is not a question of listing one's organizational affiliations as evidence of acceptance by the majority culture.[1]

The integration of middle class ethnics and whites has been achieved on many of the significant indicators such as housing availability, school preference, jobs, and opportunities. Few are barred simply because of ethnicity. What counts today is ability to pay one's way. It is fully understood that substantial discrimination is still being faced by minority persons, but overall it seems to be diminishing. Perhaps this is due to governmental programs which officially discourage it.

The size of the ethnic lower class is problematic. It comprises up to 85 percent of the ethnic population.[2] The middle class alone is able to take advantage of the opportunities of the melting pot. Each ethnic group has its "Uncle Toms," or traitors to the ethnic cause. Economically, ethnic status means lower class or poverty.

How to rapidly replace the ethnic lower class, or at least radically reduce the size of it? Disadvantaged ethnics claim the allegiance of those who are more successful and therefore in the melting pot. But allegiance based on ethnicity becomes an indefensible strategy when impediments to complete functioning in the mainstream are removed. Appeals to ethnic membership lose their force when overt discrimination is no longer a legal reality.

Throughout the history of America, ethnic status has meant social disability. It has connoted some special condition such as the inability to speak enough English to understand job or school instructions. It has meant the name calling of ethnic children at school. Parents and children, who are at different degrees of assimilation, have been torn apart because of the persistence of the ethnicity of one or the other. Ethnicity has meant social restriction, limited mobility, and placement in economic niches.[3]

But there have been efforts to redefine ethnicity so that it moves from the status of handicap to the beautiful. This is being accomplished in various ways. Some social psychologists attempt to shift the argument away from ethnicity as a disability by claiming that there are primordial urges in man to seek out and to be with his own kind. Harold Isaacs makes such a claim in his *Idols of the Tribe*.[4] Another concept widely used to account for the bunching of groups by ethnic status is Franklin H. Giddings's "consciousness of king."[5] It is sociologically similar to the folk adage "Birds of a feather flock together." William Lloyd Warner, and his school, believed that caste[6] could explain black-white relations in America, as it does in India. The concept of "soul" is also exclusionary in that its mystique derives from the idea that its meaning can only be understood by persons with black skins and former slave status.

These attempts at redefining ethnicity may encourage ethnic groups to forget their disabilities, though some are no longer disabled, and concentrate on their ethnicity as a positive social feature.

In the late 1960s and early 1970s there was a shift away from defining ethnic groups as discriminated, unassimilated groups. They were transformed, by an incredible logic, from groups with a multiplicity of deficiencies to groups whose cultures merited the greatest respect, emulation, and preservation. Depressed groups, such as the Cajuns of the swamps and bayous of Louisiana, unemployed, subsisting mainly off their highly-spiced beans, rice, crawfish tails, and tourism, were now touted as having very beautiful and preservable cultures. St. Louis Poles, without much training in either generation, limited largely to near menial blue collar work, are now told by their ethnic spokespersons to find strength and beauty in their intracultural lives. They remain highly circumscribed by their limited skills, experiences, and outlooks.

Social scientists use the existing norms to assess the status of various groups and assign labels of pathology to those too far from the mean. This never constitutes a blanket indictment of any culture, for there are always members whose achievements are on a par with, and frequently exceed, those of the majority group. Modally, however, it could be said that a group deviating far, negatively, from the norm could properly be labeled as pathological. Goffman observes that sometimes individuals or a category are expected to act the part which the label connotes.[7]

Ethnicity and minority status have never been beautiful as total ways of life in America. They have always been considered strange, different, weird, offensive, and pathological. Some traits of ethnic culture, such as the cuisine of the southern and eastern Europeans, the music of the Latins, and the rhythms and athletic abilities of some black Americans, are highly praised. Every group probably has two or three cultural specialties it can display and gain applause for, but none can elaborate a complete cultural package for itself alone without serious challenge from the majority and significant elements of other groups.

The basic thesis of this chapter is that assimilation means the ability to participate fully in society without penalty for ascribed status. Thus a small number of minority group members have always been able to take advantage of societal offerings and, in that sense, they were assimilated. Lower class persons of whatever ethnicity are not assimilated because they do not have access to the desirable societal offerings.

In America, when one opts for ethnic status, he automatically cuts himself off from the strength of the main culture and is thrown back upon weakness. Being ethnic means limiting rather than broadening experiences and resources. The ethnic group requires practically all of one's psychic energy. Accordingly, the ethnic person has little time for anything other than his ethnicity or consequences of it. Being ethnic is a full-time job; one in which he is obsessed not only with the shortcomings of other groups, but also with those of his own group.

An ethnic group does not permit its members to associate with persons outside that ethnicity on an equal basis. The group, sensing its weaknesses, seeks to control the activities of its members to prohibit defection. Ridicule, accusation of disloyalty, and other pressures are used to force individuals to associate only with people from their ethnic group. The ethnic group is an aggregation in which members are treated neither uniformly nor fairly. Under the guise of loyalty to the group, many individuals are kept from realizing their best qualities. Ethnic living is more like living in jail. Ethnicity programs one for less than all society has to offer. It is like a millstone about one's social neck.

6

PLURALISTIC CULTURE
OR PLURALISTIC PEOPLE?

"Cultural pluralism," as used in actual and academic social science, seems to mean ethnic pluralism. But logically and practically the two are not equivalent. Culture can be shared, transmitted, and the culture of one group is accessible to another. Special people are not required to transmit or preserve a special culture. Culture may be retained in various forms. Visual media, books, and monuments are important ways of preserving the culture of a group, as any librarian or historian will verify. But cultural authenticity is not always possible. Few groups have been able to preserve their old ways with 100 percent authenticity while participating in the mainstream. A minority tradition is modified and weakened over time as people socialized in different ways try to carry it out.

But preservation of culture through pluralism perpetuates particular ethnic groups and races. Since race preservation is not required to perpetuate culture, the cultural pluralism argument resolves into a racist imperative which indirectly becomes an apology for the status quo. Pluralism in America has never been the cultural ideal. E pluribus unum, the national motto, is a clear expression of the ideal of the melting pot. America, founded on a basic concept of human equality, can be diverted from this ideal through the teachings of the separatists of any racial, political, or academic stripe.

The direct descendants of a cultural tradition are not required to carry forward that tradition. If a tradition is important to a nation or country, it may be carried on by any group. For example, the Boy Scouts may feel the lore of the Indian is necessary to the making of a good scout. Consequently, the culture of the Indian, deemed necessary for scout development, is instilled into boys, not by Indians but by scouts representing a variety of ethnicities. No small group of Indians is kept around so that scouts may directly observe them to appreciate their culture and skills.

If Irish culture is important, one does not have to be Irish in order to appreciate it. In America probably more non-Irish celebrate St. Patrick's Day than Irish. The Mardi Gras has become a part of the general American culture, and its French connection in no way suggests that there are Frenchmen around who alone understand the meaning of Mardi Gras.

Likewise, if the music of black slaves of America is considered an important cultural tradition, obviously one would not want to keep the institution of slavery so that blacks might continue to produce mournful or jubilee music. Black folk music is sung in every church in America at some time or other, and "soul" food is prepared as a general course by nonblacks whose numbers run into the millions. No dance would be complete without music from the black repertoire. Black culture had an impact on the general culture, was accepted by it, at least in part, and is carried on by the general culture, not exclusively and absolutely by black people. If all blacks suddenly were removed from American life (and we cannot envision this happening), black culture would survive because it is implanted within the general cultural traditions of America and the world. It is not necessary that lineal descendants of a tradition perpetuate that tradition.

Don Sieger, of the sociology faculty at the University of Arkansas, remarked to me in 1976 that there may be confusion between the concepts of pluralistic culture and pluralistic people. It is not often clear that the two may be separate. Pluralistic cultures have existed for centuries. Local variations in social organization, lifestyles, attitudes, and values are inevitable because people do not have equivalent experiences. Isolation over a period of time accounts for more pronounced cultural differences. The same process, isolation, imposed by geography, culture, or law, finally produces a pluralistic people, or so-called ethnic groups. Different isolated people, even though ethnically homogeneous, have different cultures, and different culture is at bottom a plea for different people. People become different when they have a different culture, and because they have a different culture they are different people. The reasoning is circular. It therefore becomes difficult to eradicate a culture, because the people who are the carriers of that culture would have to be eradicated, according to this logic. Culture and people are conceptually intertwined.

By using "people" and "culture" interchangeably the pluralist argument for separate cultures becomes an argument for separate peoples, which would not change their order in the stratification system. Pluralism does not recognize the equality of cultures. Majority cultural representatives know it will be many years before minority groups can compete on equal terms with the majority group. It is therefore the separatist plan to extend inequalities already present. The advocates of pluralism may be considered ideological shotgun riders in that they are providing cover for the separatist position by assuring theoretical and ideological justification for separation.

Americans do not recognize different cultures as equals. Though many cultures are tolerated, they are not equal. The number of hillbilly records sold does not establish mountain folk music on par with the classics; nor does drag racing compare with tennis or golf. Soul food and creole gumbo, though highly appreciated in all sections of the country, do not compete seriously with the dishes of English and continental derivation after which the American diet is modeled. Sanctified and snake charming churches cannot religiously represent America as do Presbyterian, Episcopalian, or Lutheran churches. American culture is made up of many ingredients, but the major flavor is English, which remains the cultural base of the majority of the people, including the black population. The sole official language is English—or has been until very recent concessions by such federal agencies as the Bureau of the Census.

There may be sincerity in the heart of the pluralist majority person who feels that minority culture merits preservation without modification. But his is an emotional position unsupported by clear logic. As we have shown, a minority culture becomes an argument for minority people. America has not been successful in selectively accepting the culture of minority groups. Even the dances and songs of ethnic Americans are not appreciated as expressions of the art, sorrows, and joys of a highly valued people. Majority Americans take on the role of ethnics and experience the emotional release they believe ethnics do. In a sense they are exploiting the culture for their own emotional benefit. Their appreciation of ethnic culture does not increase as a result of their temporarily acting as ethnics.

It is not in agreement with the Constitution for any group to be exclusive purely by race, even if race is accorded another name. Since ethnicity tends to accommodate particular groups and to exclude others, it has the practical effect of a racial group. It is a symbol to which others have no access. Yet all cultural symbols must be open to all qualified individuals.

Culture may be arranged in any order. There may be specific linguistic tastes, dress, and religious beliefs. But the people who acquire them cannot with impunity be selected by arbitrary criteria of ascription. Thus if Poles want a Polish language club, non-Poles must be welcome if the club is to avoid being stigmatized as one exclusive by nationality. Cultural symbols are not the sole property of any ethnic group.

Although there may be many cultures, distribution through them must not be on an ethnic basis. East Indians, for example, will be in violation if they try to use Yankee Stadium for an affair from which non-Indians are barred. Yankee Stadium is private industry, but it functions as a public symbol. Martin Luther King, Jr., could not use the Washington Monument mall as a meeting place for thousands if they were to be exclusively black. Specific ethnic groups cannot be matched with specific cultures, for to do so would have the effect of segregation. But the churches of America are largely, though not wholly, in that posture. It is uncertain whether some are gaining tax advantages while maintaining segregated memberships.

Our basic idea is that cultural symbols cannot be controlled exclusively by one group for one group. All culture must be open to all who wish to participate, and those not wishing to participate must not be forced to do so. In this way ethnic and racial groups become more equitably distributed throughout the cultures. We suggest a variety of cultures of independent and parallel status being crosscut by a single people differentiated broadly by social class. The people would be mixed throughout the cultures, limiting the identification of specific ethnic groups with specific cultural symbols.

7

ETHNIC COMMUNITIES

The ethnic community is largely the product of contradictory forces, acceptance and rejection, which originate in the majority society and are directed toward immigrants. The status community, by contrast, emerges when status equals, capitalizing on internal differences of their society, close their ranks against outsiders of inferior or superior status.[1] The ethnic community, as a minority or guest element in American society, has been partly closed off from the life of the host community. It is a contradiction to the melting pot ideal. If it continues, full participation in the wider community cannot be expected by its members.

Once formed, the ethnic community moves toward closure which is reinforced by the prejudice of the majority. On the ladder of status, the ethnic communities are at the bottom and the prestigious ones at the top. Only in rare cases have immigrants been able to come to America and initially form communities of higher status than those of the local people whom they join. The selective immigration to America of East Indians in the high status professions of medicine, engineering, and academics may allow them to move toward becoming a status community based on their Old World cultural exclusiveness.[2] But it remains to be seen whether they can form a permanent community of higher prestige and status than the general run of American citizens. Iverson notes:

A status community forms when a group of natives develops a sense of honor and a style of life which sets them apart from the majority. It characteristically forms at the upper levels of society, as a monopolistic joining of elitist individuals whose common aim is to consolidate their access to values of privilege, influence, and wealth. It cultivates snobbery and is regarded by outsiders with mixed feelings of resentment and admiration.[3]

The idea of cultural pluralism can be seen and even tested graphically by an examination of communities found in various parts of the U.S. In the late 1800s it was believed that different groups could best find their identities in their separate communities and were encouraged to develop their own towns and living areas. The many immigrants settled in self-contained groups throughout the country and tried to reconstruct the ways of life of their old countries. Wherever a group of a particular religious or linguistic ethnicity could get together, they tried to form a community on that basis. In the East the Dutch, Germans, Amish, and Mormons staked out space. In the Midwest the Swedes, Danes, and Norwegians; in the West the Chinese, Japanese, and Mexicans congregated in slums. The blacks, Jews, and English fought it out for space in the cities, large and small. Each group, incredibly, though it could build its own world without major association with other groups. Today, while many of the older immigrant groups have assimilated, or at least reduced their reliance on group loyalty, other groups have not done so, and there are some visible consequences.

The ethnic communities and towns were founded as reactions to the racism so prevalent before and after the Civil War era. The failure of the government to enforce the rights of citizenship of all Americans led them to seek peace and happiness among their own people by establishing towns catering to their ethnicity. Some of these towns were not even founded by members of the ethnic group which they were supposed to serve. Many ethnic towns were speculative schemes proposing to rescue ethnic peoples by providing them with land at costs they could afford. The Exodusters to Kansas and Oklahoma were led there by the lure of cheap land where they could escape the sharecrop system of near peonage built up after the Civil War. The Indians were subjected to a similar fate. Their confinement to reservations began in the early 1800s, and by the latter decade of the century they were concentrated largely in poor areas of the Midwest, Southwest, and far western mountains.

These attempts at settling people according to their ethnicity, and not giving them status as citizens, resulted in the decaying communities we see today. With no significant ties to the main society, the ethnic settlements are like homes in a community which must maintain their private water and sewer systems. None of these communities was founded on a fundamental belief in cultural pluralism; their founding was a reaction to the rejection of their cultural and ethnic differences. And through-out the country, where ethnic communities were founded, they remain outside the system of respect and prosperity characteristic of the main areas where the people are integrated into the context of full citizenship.

Ethnic communities are still found throughout America, but they are all dying. In central Oklahoma the little town of Prague was started by Czechoslovakians nearly one hundred years ago. Today Prague is like any other small town, with the usual main street and its service facilities. The only reminder that the town was formerly made up of Czech immigrants is its recently established Czech Inn. Whether the inn is authentic or merely a ploy to attract customers is not known. There was opposition to the settlement of the Czechs in Prague, but they persisted and built institutions which catered to their needs. But Prague was affected by outside elements. Language was first to be contested, and soon Czech was no longer the main language of the area. As the children and youth within a generation became fluent in English, intermarriage and immigration so changed the character of the Czech community that in a generation or less it was hardly visible as an ethnic enclave. Many Czech names are still seen on mailboxes, but the number is small compared to the English ones. Prague had to give up its ethnic identity or face decay, the fate of other small ethnic communities.

Illustrations may be found in the examples of all-black and all-Indian towns in Oklahoma. All-black Boley, Oklahoma, was founded around 1890.[4] Its purpose was to provide an opportunity for black people to develop to the fullest of their abilities within the context of black leadership and encouragement. The town reached a population of three or four thousand before 1940 but started to decline rapidly after America's entry into World War 2. At its zenith, Boley had schools, churches, stores of several varieties, and modest homes of which the citizenry were proud. It had no industry; subsistence and cotton farming were the principal occupations.

Today Boley is in the throes of decline. The stores of the town have long been boarded up, and aside from several beer-drinking places, the business of the town has all but ceased. Buildings are vacant and crumbling, their free-standing brick walls a hazard to the children who run through them in innocent play. The Boley Rodeo is an annual event which is said to attract several thousand spectators. Principal employment for the residents of Boley is at the State School for Juveniles.

Some 130 miles away in eastern Oklahoma is Stilwell, a small town in the heart of the Cherokee Nation. Stilwell and Boley are not strictly comparable, for while Boley has almost no white families, Stilwell has many, though the population is mainly of Indian extraction. Boley and Stilwell have high rates of unemployment, and exceptional poverty; each tries to capitalize on a way of life which is long gone. While Boley's few stores are operated by black owners, in Stilwell the pattern of ethnic storekeeping is less prevalent. Whites are in charge of the stores, and Indians are the helpers. Both towns have a local option for the purchase of beer on Sundays; Boley sells no Sunday beer while Stilwell does. Boley receives some federal and state funds for the support of water and fire protection, as does Stilwell. Additionally, Stilwell Indians may be on the Bureau of Indian Affairs rolls, which qualifies them for certain types of support as reservation Indians.

Tontitown, Arkansas, is a small, predominantly Italian community of some three hundred persons. It contains one street of stores, beer parlors, and restaurants specializing in Italian cuisine. It has a parish school and church. The community was settled nearly eight-five years ago by a large band of Italians who took up grape farming in the flatter portion of Washington County in the Arkansas Ozarks. Today only the oldest settlers or their descendants speak Italian, and Tontitown is hardly distinguishable as an Italian community. The town is about three miles out of Springdale, Arkansas, a city of some twenty thousand. Springdale, Fayetteville, Siloam Springs, and Rogers, all within some twenty-five miles of Tontitown, provide the major places of employment for Tontitown residents. Each year there is a festival which attracts thousands of persons, most of whom are descendants, for entertainment and spaghetti eating, and the crowning of Queen Concordia.[5]

Vienna and Freeburg are small, originally German towns in central Missouri. Neither has a population of more than five hundred. Farming was formerly the principal occupation in each vicinity, but today most of the residents work in Jefferson City some fifteen or twenty miles away. The Catholic churches are the only evidence of ethnic identity in these towns aside from some German names. Some German is still spoken but only by the oldest people. Neither Vienna nor Freeburg has any industry.

Along the Mississippi River between St. Louis and Memphis, French communities such as St. Genevieve have lost their identity except as place names. In none of them is there anything other than the barest reminder that French culture once flourished there. The largest remnant of French culture in the U.S. seems to be the Cajun culture of Louisiana. But only a few of the Cajuns who claim cosmopolitan status identify with the culture. To be Cajun does not command high status even in Louisiana, for most Cajuns are poor, uneducated, and are believed to be involved in the mysterious culture of the Louisiana bayous and swamps.

The following study of the decline of two ethnic communities in central Arkansas illustrates some of the processes at work which handicapped their development. Detail is given to show the ways in which some concepts are used in analyses of pluralistic communities.

Conway is at the geographical center of Arkansas. Today it is a city of about 20,000, with three colleges and substantial industry. On its north, south, and eastern borders are found man-made lakes which have helped spur the economy through water sports and tourist trade. On the west, the Arkansas River is bridged to connect with Perry County on the other side.

Whites make up about 90 percent of the population and blacks about 10 percent. Subsumed under the white population were the two major white ethnic communities, the Germans and the Italians. The foreign born numbered .5 percent of the 25,880 persons in Faulkner County in 1940.[6] The German and Italian foreign born were about 100 persons strong in each of their communities. Their American born children would raise their number by a factor of three, perhaps, making the communities around 300 each, or some 600 persons in all.

Old settlers of each community arrived in Faulkner County during the 1870s. They acquired land at the prevailing low prices and began life anew as farmers. After establishing households the two communities began to build their basic institutions. A permanent Catholic church was one of the first requirements. Old World hostilities between the Germans and Italians prohibited their attending mass together, though the two communities could afford only one church and priest. Early American priests were bilingual, having studied in Europe, mastering several languages. Most of their parishioners, however, were fluent only in English.

Members of these communities fell into the same occupational niches, having brought over from Europe common skills. Each saw opportunities in farming and winemaking, and soon enmity developed between the groups as they sought to control the winemaking industry. The German and Italian farmers held adjoining acreage in several cases. Both raised grapes, using their large family members as the principal labor force in the fields. As the two groups became relatively prosperous, they tended to hire labor from the nearby black community. They very seldom exchanged family labor, even during the peak harvesting seasons.

The Italians were soon driven out of winemaking, first by their failure to consolidate their buying power. They failed to cooperate in the establishment of a winemaking plant which met state health department standards. They continued in agricultural work, but it became increasingly unattractive to the younger people. Also, after a generation, family size started to fall, thus depriving the families of the labor required to run the farms on an economical basis. Later they attempted to specialize in the raising of hogs with the idea of establishing a butchery and meat-packing plant. They found this line of work blocked by the Germans who by now had gained a foothold in all aspects of the food industry.

The Germans sought to secure their livelihood by controlling much of the food industry in the county. They raised food on their farms and sold it in stores they owned. Some Germans monopolized the sale of produce from door to door, after thoroughly undercutting the Italians and the single black competitor in the field.

Through the 1940s German names were found on the signs of the largest food stores in Conway. Germans also controlled lesser stores. In some other Arkansas towns the tendency toward control of the food industry by Germans was noted, not only in retail selling, but in warehousing and distribution as well.

World War 2 helped to break up the ethnic communities of small towns such as Conway. It created nonfarm work opportunities for family members. The technology of farming was altered during and soon after the war, and less hand labor was required. Girls and boys with ethnic backgrounds found their way into respectable white collar occupations. Their mobility freed them from the constricting choices imposed by their local communities. This shift of ethnic people exposed them to other values and no doubt attuned them to the limitations of their own outlooks so that they became sensitive to rather than proud of their ethnic memberships.

Probably the enormous expansion of the war effort broke up monopolies and ethnic arrangements as many businesses and industries important to the war effort had to be effectively managed with winning the war as the primary goal. The experience workers gained during the war was valuable afterwards. Farmers and businessmen often acquired the knowledge, capital, and connections to undertake larger economic operations. Small, family-owned, or ethnically-run farms and businesses had difficulty in succeeding. More and more citizens sought work in the larger industries and businesses. Government employment opportunities increased, and ethnic peoples took their share of such jobs.

The war and its aftermath devastated the German and Italian communities of Conway, though they had probably been in a state of decline even before. Today the Catholic community consists of little more than the parish church and school as physical reminders of its former status. The children have practically disappeared into the public schools, and ethnic languages are scarcely heard. Only old folks can reminisce in an Old World tongue. The large family feasts associated with marriages are seldom held. Italians and Germans long ago married into the Anglo communities.

Not only was there conflict between the Italians and Germans who placed negative labels on each other, but a system of rank existed within each community. German Protestants had little to do with German Catholics, and German Jews not connected with agriculture did not mingle with either. There was no synagogue or visible institution which catered to the Jewish community, small as it was. Little Rock was 32 miles away and the means of transportation too underdeveloped to permit frequent trips for other than business purposes. The few Jews of German nationality evidently threw in their lot with the Protestant Anglos, who controlled most of the status and wealth in the town and county.

One of the victims of modernization was the institution of the patriarchy. In one illustrative extended family, the grandfather had reached over 70 years of age and the older son over 30. The father wanted the sons to follow the traditional occupation of farming. The oldest son wanted to escape it. The son established a winery, in direct competition with the father, soon driving him out of business. The old man promptly disinherited the son of the family land and forbade other sons and daughters from fraternizing with him. By now the son had married a hill woman of English background who had no knowledge of German culture. She joined her husband in castigating German culture, the Catholic religion, and the priesthood whenever she could.

When the county went dry, the son continued to make money by selling wine and whiskey illegally while accumulating substantial farm acreage. He spent considerable time in the black community at homes whose members were known to fancy the high life. The children were not raised as ethnic Germans and maintained only minimal ties to the Catholic church. Eventually the children all married outside the German community and found their status outside of Conway.

After the death of the foreign-born grandfather, this extended family went into rapid dissolution. Property was divided and some of it sold. Eventually the large tract of land held by the German family and regarded as the center of the community was sold to the state for the building of a colony for handicapped children.

The Italians suffered essentially the same fate. Their farms were, in general, smaller and more poorly run than those of the Germans. They were unable to pay competitive wages for farm labor. They sold out first, some taking up with relatives in other counties and others casting their lots within the general environment. As in the German case, Italian sons rebelled against their fathers' wishes, refusing appeals to their filial obedience.

Neither the German nor the Italian communities of Conway had strict territorial boundaries. There were informal place names such as German Lane or Pallidino's Road, but nothing which gave definition to the communities. Germans spoke broken German and Italians broken Italian in the more intimate familial settings. Mother tongues were used for issuing instructions to older ethnics but seldom in conversation with the younger people. Not much emphasis was placed on overt symbols of ethnic culture except on Sunday when the families took their turns at mass. Neither of these groups was political, in that none ran for any elective office in the town or county. Perhaps, since they maintained a separate school system, few were interested in the politics of local school elections.

Immigrants to America, in general, could not keep up their ethnic specializations as they were maintained in the Old Country. Even there they had been vulnerable to social and economic forces which they could not control, which is probably the main reason they migrated. In the new land they sought to recover their old niches but found conditions unfavorable. In America the Germans need not become butchers and farmers, the Irish policemen, and the Poles carpenters. Moreover, it became a stigma to remain too closely connected with an ethnic community. Ethnic role options were too restricting. Specialization by ethnic group was defeated early by the division of land to immigrants. Although attempts were made to settle the eastern seaboard by ethnic and religious affiliation, the revolutionary war called a halt to these decisions. The move West, across the Alleghenies and into the valley of the Ohio, drew all ethnic groups. They settled as families, trying to preserve their groups as well as they could. But the territory was too vast, and coin superseded status or origin as the basis of competition. Ethnic groups had to submerge their differences in order to deal with the hostilities and problems of the moving frontier. Indians made little distinction between Catholic or Protestant, Irish or German scalps. The labor requirements were great, and strong arms and backs were more important than social origins. "Are you willing to work?" was a more salient question than "Where are you from?" So Swede and Dane, Dutch and German, Catholic and Protestant finally settled together. Here and there blacks settled in, taking their turns at the plow or with the ox and the axe, with few people being interested in origins.

The ethnic communities of Conway failed to survive because the ethnics were no longer discriminated against and were able to find options in the larger society. There were neither real opportunities nor needs to establish symbiotic relations with other ethnic groups. No group could be protected through a restriction of jobs or opportunities.

Ethnic communities have been in a state of decline all over America, at least since World War 2. Out-migration, zoning regulations unfavorable to the ethnic group, loss of the occupational base of the community, urban renewal which treats these communities as slums, and the entry of other people with little interest in preserving the ethnic character of the neighborhood have been some factors working against them.[7]

As in the large cities, where ethnic peoples have congregated in slums, those in small towns have a very difficult time maintaining a positive identity. The ethnic community is generally not one of prosperity, nor does it command high respect in the overall community. It is a place where all the important socioeconomic indicators are low: education, occupations, housing, and living standards. These communities are an embarrassment to the general citizenry, for they remind them of the low status of separate communities. The poverty of the ethnic town is not offset by its offering of some genuine item or aspect of highly valued Old World culture. For example, it is not generally feasible to maintain Tontitown, Arkansas, merely so there there may be Italian spaghetti houses in northwest Arkansas. Similarly, it is not productive to maintain Chinatown in San Francisco or Los Angeles so that affluent Californians may drive in to secure take-home chop suey plates. Ethnic people as such have nothing else to sell but some aspect of their ethnicity, whether it be cooking, as with the Greeks, Italians, and Chinese; art, as with the American Indians; or musical and athletic talent, as with blacks unable to rise above ethnicity.

Ethnicity limits individuals to a few choices and options in comparison to those available in the mainstream. Ethnic people are too few to support ethnic enterprises, and so those who cling to ethnic living and identity are, in effect, sharply reducing their options for social mobility.

8

FROM NATIONALISM
TO MANIPULATED PLURALISM

Black nationalist activity proved that blacks are no longer afraid of white retaliation and that they cannot be subdued by psychological or physical intimidation. Nationalism provided a language with which to express contempt for the society and culture of the dominant group. But this produced within the young black from the inner city a plan of action which encouraged him to confuse anger with competence and rhetoric with achievement and also led to the conclusion that reliance on a black brotherhood was the solution to all problems.

The news media created the black nationalists Malcolm X, Eldridge Cleaver, Stokely Carmichael, and H. Rap Brown. They were to be pitted against the nationalists (racists) of the majority group. Setting up two extreme groups which could not communicate, around which America might be polarized, could only fix the outcome against the blacks, who represented only a small sample of the capacity for exerting violence and general mistreatment within the society. By endorsing the extremist position of their own nationalists, the whites could dampen the thrust for equality. That nationalist extremism cannot solve the problem of black second class citizenship has been clear to adult black leaders for many years. They have never endorsed the separatist idea but have felt that the only solution is the removal of barriers to black citizenship, a step which does not require separation or even compensatory consideration for the poorest of them.

The black power movement was significant in demonstrating the callous hypocrisy and racism of white America and served to make the black student feel angelically perfect. His contempt for the insincerity of white leaders caused him to throw up his hands and declaim the meaninglessness of achievement. He could not be taught by persons unsympathetic or ignorant of black problems. They were part of the problem.

Those who achieved, according to majority norms, were seen as uninvolved in the black struggle on any meaningful level. Refusing to go to school to have one's mind processed by white teachers or white-oriented black ones, declining to learn skills salable on the general market, and raising the awareness of blacks about their plight through street organizing, were actions interpreted as work more relevant to black liberation.

The black power movement made the angry black student believe his shortcomings were in fact strengths transmitted to him from the bedrock of black culture. Evident shortcomings in basic skills and functions were converted into strong suits which were believed capable of revolutionizing America. One prominent black poet tried to show she was doing blacks a revolutionary service by having babies without the benefit of accepted paternity. At least three generations (twelve years) of black college students were lost to the mystique of black power and the conviction that the passion and religion of blackness would open doors to them.

But the slogan "black power" was truly a psychologically liberating force in the lives of black people. Not since the 1920s and the program of Marcus Garvey had they really felt good about themselves. This good feeling led to the belief that no goal was out of reach, and many blacks, drunk with it, thought they could get along without any attachment to the mainstream. So convinced were some that emotional and psychological freedom meant actual freedom, that they disparaged any plan which involved white people in other than subordinate and manipulatee roles. The rise of Malcolm X, Robert Williams, and other fearless ghetto leaders, encouraged a generation of young blacks to shun the traditional program of working within the system and taking advantage of educational opportunities offered by the middle class community. Ironically, their orientation toward separation came at a time when it was easiest for them to achieve upward mobility through the traditional system. They so gravely agitated for change that the white community became guilt-ridden and was convinced that black objections and demands had merit. The tendency was to acknowledge the legitimacy of black demands without seriously questioning some of them. And while some whites were sincere in their reaction, many others were not and simply said give the blacks what they ask and forget about them.

This was a form of racism, for it encouraged the blacks to ask for concessions which forced them into a separatist role. Their demands were small compared to the resources of the general white community, and were relatively easy to meet. Black studies departments in colleges, for instance, did not cost much money. Six or eight black studies teachers would be a small price to pay' relative to a faculty of three or four hundred persons and thirty or more departments in a medium sized university. Separation is what many whites wanted in the first place. Black demands for their own community would ensure or forestall integration. It would be simpler to meet the demands than to have the black community press for integration into the general society. Keeping the ghetto, then, was an outcome of the "black power" movement, for it diverted action and attention from the thrust toward first class citizenship and inclusion in the mainstream.

The black ghetto, whether gilded or deprived, is evidence of the failure of America to live up to its goal of equality for all citizens. A separate black neighborhood means that processes are still at work to deny blacks first class citizenship. Black institutions—schools, churches, communities, businesses, or organizations which cater wholly to a black and separate clientele—serve as lingering reminders of the days when blacks had no rights as citizens and had to develop their own second and third class institutions. Such institutions are reaction formations, a consequence of the frustration of blacks pushing to become incorporated into the mainstream and of the persistence of racist whites in denying them that entry.

The failure of black institutions, such as business and education, reflects the increasing outside involvement of blacks who are first class citizens. Any separatist institution must appeal to the classes which lack access to the symbols of respectability. As blacks gain these symbols which indicate citizenship, they have no further use for the institutions of the black community. They may be sympathetic to the need for such institutions, but practically they do not need them, for these blacks are incorporated into the opportunity and access structures of the larger community.

Building up the black community, then, is a temporary program, one bound to lose in the long run, for there is no way to encourage blacks to remain in such a community, which all view as a product of racism. Providing blacks with better housing in their community may relieve some of the critical housing deficiencies, but really can be interpreted as delaying the day when blacks will insist on houses in a community where they will be recognized as first class citizens. Black hospitals result from a large number of blacks concentrated in a ghetto without access to the facilities taken for granted as adequate by the general white citizenry. Black schools and colleges mean there are intentions by the black and white leadership structures to retain sizable proportions of blacks in the underclasses, and such institutions must be maintained for this purpose.

Why do things always go wrong for blacks? A few years ago Laurence J. Peter, with Raymond Hull, proposed the famous "Peter Principle."[1] In their book they noted that people, in an effort to get ahead in life, rise above their levels of competence. Promotions often mean their graduation into positions for which they are inadequately prepared, psychologically or technically. They, and society, might have been better off if they had remained where they were.

Peter's logic may also be applied to the black community, whose betterment projects are always failing. In the early 1920s "buy black" programs failed and black small business could not get rolling. In the 1940s and after World War 2 attempts to clean up the ghetto led to legal attacks on restrictive covenants, which culminated in their being declared unconstitutional; but little change in residential patterns took place. Of course, blacks were not happy with their own schools, and no amount of spending to clean them up was satisfactory. The *Brown* decision of 1954 was fought for by black lawyers, for the most part, and they had to show not only that the separate schools were inferior, but that despite increased expenditures black schools were failing (these really mean the same thing). The list could be lengthened. In the 1970s, under President Nixon, black capitalism made a brief appearance on the public stage. It was rejected as more blacks tried to get jobs in those companies, agencies, and activities which formerly had discriminated. Nobody wanted work in a ghetto store as a small business employee uncertain of his weekly or monthly check.

How does all of this relate to the Peter Principle? Things go wrong when blacks are helped as blacks. Each black helped means one more on his way out of the ghetto. He does not need help to remain in the ghetto; his being there is evidence that he is not being helped. If there is massive black help, there will be massive exoduses from the ghetto and the program of help will be viewed as a failure.

The ghetto is the prison of black people. It is a place where they remain out of sight and out of mind. It is not a compromise but simply a separate living place for those people rejected by white society. Practically no legitimate institutions are developed in the ghetto, save the school and the church. Prostitution and gaming houses, bootleg whiskey places, and a few small businesses find fertile soil for development. Generally, if it is legal, it cannot be found in the ghetto. There are limited expertise, money, and hope.

Somehow the ghetto graduated to the title "black community," as if to imply that its pathological features had been transformed into something better and more desirable. Community suggests that people are living there by choice and are happy. The ghetto is presented by pluralists as a desirable place to live when in reality the pathological features remain.[2]

While a few institutions survive in the ghetto, none is viable. It is often believed that blacks do not have the skills to make their institutions function. This is not the case. In reality, there is little interest in making them viable, for to do so would confute the logic of the American system. Black institutions strive for viability only when the general system is intolerant of their quests for equal citizenship. If citizenship can be attained through access to white institutions, there is no point in maintaining separate black institutions. Such institutions are, a priori, in America, at least, evidence of the malintegration of all levels of blacks into the general social structure of the land. Ghettos cannot be made shiny enough to convince blacks that a separate life with separate status in the system is what they have been fighting for all the time. Black people are not separatists and as a whole have never approved of separatist institutions. Their commitment is to the values of integration and equality as standard members of the American citizenry. If given the opportunity to be included as a full partner in the drama of American citizenship or to develop a separate culture, however affluent it might be, the ordinary black citizen would chose the former. This would not be out of a belief that his development was inferior, or that of the major culture superior, but would hinge on his basic teachings about the value of human equality.

In America two processes have been going on simultaneously: the instilling of ethnocentrism and a sense of superiority into the general white population, while a sense of futility, helplessness, resignation, and self-hatred has been instilled into the blacks. The two groups have moved further apart and, with the help of scholarly legitimators and other reinforcers such as schools, churches, and the business sector, have encamped themselves psychologically and economically miles apart. To teach the theory of white superiority, visible evidence has been required. Whites have been allowed to live in better houses, cleaner communities, to have better jobs and more services. They needed to be kept in decision-making positions. The white lower class was to remain invisible, and those in that class were to live physically close to blacks or like the black lower class.

In the same way, blacks have been shown that they are inferior. They have been kept in ghettos, with poor and rundown housing. They have been denied medical services because their young people have been barred from training and even from practice among their own people. Their schools have been, in general, very poor, and if any black received higher formal education it was not planned, for this achievement was almost unbelievable. Black families have been chronically discouraged because a head of household could not make enough money to allow his family a respectable living standard. Social pathology reigned in the ghetto.[3]

By an incredible illogic, white establishment scholars started to say that black culture was beautiful. Black scholars had said this very early as a counter to the supremacist logic of the time, but few blacks took them seriously. Carter G. Woodson's claims about the beauty of African culture were an attempt to encourage blacks to feel positive about themselves and their backgrounds. Marcus Garvey had understood that people would not change unless they changed both their psychology and economic positions.

Once blacks started accepting the beauty of their culture, and how great its foundation was in earlier days in Africa, it was easy for white scholars to pick up the chant, even indirectly, and reinforce the ghetto dwellers in that belief. The black had been made a separate entity through a process of systematic mistreatment. The main business before America now was to make him reproduce himself so that his status would be perpetuated. This could be done by taking advantage of the incipient "black is beautiful" germ which has always existed in the ghetto. Paul Lawrence Dunbar and Langston Hughes capitalized upon it during the Harlem Renaissance. Thomas R. Cripps notes that in movies three periods are observable in regard to the portrayal of Negroes. Up until 1954 blacks were treated as a social problem. From about 1950 to the early 1960s they began to take on character but retained a heavy dose of the "Rastus" image. In the 1960s they were filmed as fully articulated characters.[4] Blyden Jackson's examination of Negro fiction expresses the idea very clearly. Slum living, in Richard Wright's *Native Son*, Ralph Ellison's *Invisible Man*, Ann Petry's *The Street*, and Willard Motley's *Knock on Any Door*, all show that talent and "goodness" may form and flower in the ghetto.[5] The few people who rose to prominence were held up as evidence of what could be achieved in the black community. Joe Louis, Jesse Owens, and Sugar Ray Robinson became legitimate symbols of the physical prowess young men needed to cultivate in order to survive in the ghetto. Numbers kings, flamboyant preachers, high class prostitutes, and pimps living lives of luxury were envied.

The few blacks who are now in secure positions in middle class life have found themselves in the dilemma of advocating a position for the masses which they themselves would reject. By claiming to relate to the struggle for black improvement, they hope to relate to the masses. But poor blacks are legitimately disgruntled about their unenviable positions in the system. They suffer many disabilities and hardships. They are limited by lack of mobility, options, training, and skills. They are consigned to very poor sections of cities and towns and see no way out of their predicament.

In order to show they are not abandoning the struggle, middle class blacks tend academically, but not physically, to identify with those left behind in the ghetto. This enables them to offer programs which call for blacks to get themselves together through their own efforts, by pulling themselves up by their bootstraps, and by capitalizing on ethnicity.

The dilemma is: How can one ensconced in a middle class position relate to a category mired in poverty? If the middle class black does not relate, he is accused of being an "Uncle Tom." If he does relate, he is called an "Oreo," one who is black on the outside but white on the inside. In either case limits are placed on his ability to be effective in working for blacks in a context wider than a localized and immediate ethnic group.

Considerable attention has been focused on the black problem because it is the prototype of all American ethnic problems and processes of change. A few conclusions can be derived from the similarities of these cases. Middle class ethnics are an embarrassment to their fellows because they prove the weakness of the pluralistic ethnic culture. The culture cannot accommodate achievement in a wide range of fields. The ethnic subculture can encourage indigenous people to persist only in a few areas: art, music, entertainment, and small retail shopkeeping. Opportunities are found outside, in the mainstream, not in the ethnic communities where little mobility is possible.

But this is the type of setting which some younger scholars are recommending for substantial numbers of inner city people. *They* have transcended the narrowness of ethnicity to gain the skills, talent, and orientation to function in the mainstream. *They* are living in the integrated suburbs and communities and interacting with an educated worldly clientele, experiencing many of the things considered "good" which the larger society has to offer. Yet they suggest to the general masses that there is something beautiful and strong within the ghetto culture. These "escapees" of the ghetto take first class citizenship for granted and resent any insinuation of the relevance of ethnicity in their social placement. They insist on believing that they owe their position to brains and opportunity and not to ethnicity. The hiring of minority members in formerly closed positions tells more about the opening of those positions than about the distribution of brainpower. While intelligence is normally distributed, opportunity is not, and the two are sometimes confused.

Communicating with the impoverished throngs in the ghettos is a problem because "you are either in the category helping us to get out, or you are outside helping to keep us in." When you move out, you become part of the system of oppression. The circle is vicious. Consequently, a successful ethnic must return, even symbolically, to visit the ghetto, eat some pigs' feet (or some lox and bagels), dig some Ray Charles (or peasant folk songs), drink a beer on the drag (or a draught of strong bootleg black beer which "only my folks know how to make"), wear a dashiki now and then (or don a skullcap and try to read the ethnic newspaper). All these actions remind him of his roots and cause him to reflect upon his own relative success compared to the enduring struggles and poverty of those left behind. But as quickly as he completes his symbolic battery charge, he returns to his integrated world, ignoring, if not completely forgetting, the struggle of his acquaintances for the elements of human decency.

Such people understand that there is little vitality in the separate ghetto culture; only pathology. But they are unwilling to say to their fellows, "In order to be effective you must acquire the tools to join the mainstream, for there is little positive to be won in the ghetto." And there is little hope for self-fulfillment in the separation of an ethnically distinct society.

9

SEPARATISM IN THE SOCIAL SCIENCES

When the several academic disciplines which have entered the debate on cultural pluralism are grouped together, social science becomes most notable. The subject matter is no doubt most natural for them since culture, the learned, shared products of human association, is one of their principal concepts. Not many decades ago scholars trained in the quantitative sciences tried to conclude the separatism of cultures by arguing from anthropometric data.[1] They purported to prove the differences of races which then exhibited differences of culture when separated for long periods.[2] Today, scholars are replowing much of that same ground, this time using any means possible, even invoking the findings of genetics and biology, to support cultural pluralism and thereby justify the separation of races. This chapter discusses how social science has become involved in the debate on cultural pluralism and how it is providing logic which will be used by the believers in pluralism to support pluralist policies.

Social science is like any other other science in that its findings have greater believability when they come from eminent persons in the field. Typically, an event happens, and an institutional or social response to a pattern occurs. In due time the event or pattern is analyzed by some member of the social science community. Many patterns go unanalyzed because no individual or foundation is willing to spend the time or money required to do the study. There is seldom great urgency about a social science analysis unless it is an official response to some crisis, such as the wave of riots of the 1960s, to provide temporary relief to a vexed and frightened public. Social science studies can wait another day or they can be shelved upon completion if it is not politically expedient to release their contents. Much social science, therefore, is not politically sanctioned in that the research has not been approved and funded by some political or quasi-political agency. Small-scale research often does not have the political visibility of the large-scale, well-funded studies and therefore may be more easily overlooked or disqualified because of alleged methodological or theoretical biases and limitations. The political implications of the findings may be hidden at the bottom of refusal. Social scientists, because of their limited opportunities to complete current studies, must frequently analyze from a distance, from relatively limited primary group studies or secondary sources. Consider the implications of several black withdrawal movements. Marcus Garvey's back to Africa movement of 1915 to the 1920s was perhaps the first twentieth-century movement mounted by blacks to solve the problem of America's unfair treatment of them. Although posing withdrawal as a solution and generating a great deal of pomp and pageantry, Garvey's program was lacking as a serious challenge to the majority of blacks. Thousands gave verbal and some financial support to Garvey, but few felt ready to abandon promising futures in America for the uncertainties of life in Africa.[3] While Garvey dreamed of past and future black greatness in Africa, most American blacks continued their relentless movement toward a middle class existence, however precarious, within the mainstream, or at least close to it.

The next withdrawal movement of scale to reach public attention was that of the Black Muslims, otherwise known as the Nation of Islam. C. Eric Lincoln, in 1961, then a relatively unknown social science scholar, brought the Muslims to public attention. Since the early 1920s the Muslims had been pressing ahead with the establishment of their institutions, stores, bookshops, schools, newspapers, and rehabilitation programs for prisoners. If noticed at all, they were regarded as a curiosity by social scientists and even by black people within their community. This continued until about 1961 when Lincoln published his *The Black Muslims in America.* Lincoln saw the Muslims as a religious group. As such they were understandable and more easily placed within the tradition of black American behavior and social protest. By 1962, with the publication of E. U. Essien-Udom's work *Black Nationalism,* the Muslims were regarded more frequently as a separatist, racist, militant organization. Some whites and blacks were frightened into realizing the potential danger of having black people so thoroughly alienated from the general society.

Until the Muslims openly declared their hatred for America, there was no important theoretical support among grass roots academics for ethnic separatism. The boldness of the Muslim assertion and their great confidence in their ability to live comfortably with minimum ties to the white community was a theme not recently heard by Americans. A nation within America seemed quite out of context politically and socially, for more people have always wanted to enter America, even with its multiplicity of problems, than to withdraw from it. It was far from the thoughts of most Americans that any group would choose any other way of life than that of mainstream America if given the option. The pull of American middle class culture was too great, and only thoroughly and religiously alienated people would reject it. As long as groups retained some hope of participating in the system and reaping some of its rewards on an equal basis, there would be no serious thought given to separatism. The Muslims taught that there are groups who say they hate America's ways and who do not wish to become identified with it. But the Muslims were not allowed to form a genuinely separate culture, just as Marcus Garvey had been imprisoned rather than allowed to succeed with a separatist or withdrawal movement.

The Muslims, perhaps the first of the groups to be seen as separatist, were considered cruel, dangerous, and misguided persons because they said they saw white America as evil, all white people as devils, and wanted no part of either. Moreover, they would be violent with any person who crossed them. They would gladly live separately and from their own resources. As the years passed and more analyses of the Black Muslims were made, mainly from the writings of C. Eric Lincoln and later Essien-Udom, the conclusion became almost unalterable that the Muslims were a hate group comparable to the Ku Klux Klan. Twenty years after there were few fresh studies of the Muslims but the conclusions remained the same: Their separatist beliefs and hatred for white people were dangerous for the country, and the Muslims should be closely watched. Whether the Muslims were truly a hate group, or whether their hatred was created by the media is an interesting issue.

As long as the Muslims were seen as a religious group, they could be understood and more easily placed within the tradition of black American behavior. Their separatism would then lose its significance. But when they, through social science analysis, became defined as nationalistic their behavior became frightening and unacceptable. The Muslims were different from other blacks. They were all business. They inspired fear, asking no quarter and giving none. They were seen as law-abiding, mysterious, nontalkative believers in self-help, and they were resisters of welfare payments or any other identification with "Negroes."

Although social scientists today use the Muslims as the prime example of black separatism, they seldom offer thorough analyses of Muslim programs and social meanings. But separatist-minded scholars became quite impressed with the Muslim program. Soon after Essien-Udom's book on the Muslims was published, the Glazer–Moynihan volume *Beyond the Melting Pot* appeared. If a few hundred thousand blacks could find benefit in a separatist logic, though they were an insignificant fraction of the millions of blacks, perhaps independent cultures and peoples might yet have a chance in America. In a few short years it became academically fashionable to rediscover the strength of ethnicity and pluralism in various communities.

During the 1960s the urban riots and the Vietnam War so polarized America that some social scientists began to talk about genuine separation as black communities became known as colonies instead of ordinary ghettos. The groundwork had already been laid for acceptance of the doctrine of separation some years earlier. Antiassimilationist groups have always existed in America, but the assimilationists were more numerous and more powerful in that assimilation encompassed the ideology of the country while separatism did not. It was more difficult to translate separatism into political policy than assimilationism because, probably, the majority of people are greater believers in assimilation than in separatism. For years the social distance scales first brought out by E. S. Bogardus in the early 1920s showed that some American rhetoric was separatist.[4] But wherever openings could be found to integrate blacks, without too seriously compromising the system, they were accepted. Integration proceeded faster in the North than in the South. Blacks who were well off were assimilated before poor ones, and those blacks fair-skinned enough to pass received opportunities more frequently than those more visibly black.[5]

A reversal of the assimilationist doctrine would seem to be the intention of pluralists, who must logically be identified with the separatists. Through repetition of the findings and logic of writers such as Novak, Moynihan, Glazer, Greeley, and a few blacks such as James Banks of the University of Washington, separatism has become almost automatically accepted. The theory itself now seems more easily justified. Social science findings now become ammunition for the beginning and defense of ethnic programs of very committed separatists and eventually become the basis of government policy in the ethnic field. The separatist policy then becomes supported by law and directive and becomes difficult to displace. It assumes a quality of "rightness" even though it is erected upon highly debatable premises.

There are several varieties of social science now participating in the pluralism debate. Each perspective seeks to show that pluralism is derived from its orientation. Earlier, in the chapter "Theories and Pluralism," it was argued that conflict sociology implies pluralism,[6] but pluralism fits most easily into the conservative or functionalist category, as we shall see. Conservative or functionalist social science sees stability and order as the central goals of society, even if order is achieved at the expense of the rights of other citizens. Around the turn of the century William Graham Sumner could declare, defending the cake of custom: "The mores make anything right."[7] Sumner's conservatism was so profound he could not understand that power defines the mores.

Perhaps the most powerful of the conservative practices is that of caste, which is clearly separatist in its emphasis. Caste was found in its purest form in India. It is a system of hereditary social ascription. Mobility in a caste society is slight. By contrast, a class system is more open—status depends mostly upon individual achievement. Positions in a class society are open to all who wish to compete for them. Lloyd Warner and his students tried unsuccessfully to show that black Americans are a caste.[8] Much research has been generated around this concept. Gerald Berreman has probably been the most prominent spokesman within the past decade or so who supports the caste position as it relates to blacks.[9] He sees caste as an alternative to assimilation or the melting pot.

Caste and class thinking dominated sociological thought from the 1930s through the 1950s. Caste lost some of its force and class gained.[10] Scholars overlooked evidence contradicting the caste position but were never able to prove the existence of a true class system in America. Caste and class both were based on conditioned fear, according to those advocating full citizenship for blacks. There was nothing caste-like about going to segregated schools, drinking from segregated fountains, or riding in the back of the bus. Second class citizenship was based on a simple breaking of the law by those charged with upholding it. But social scientists, trying to make their theory agree with both their ideology and current practice supported by law, chose the caste explanation. So southern race relations were described and discussed as caste relations, which became the accepted interpretation of such relations in the South.

Social scientists have sometimes had difficulty in interpreting the meanings of social events. They concluded, for example, that Muslims would rather be separated from whites than be fairly and equitably integrated with them. They overlook that all people who understand the history of ethnic separation and mistreatment in America see the Muslim reaction as one of many a humiliated people might adopt. A conclusion that their ideology is separatist, independent of the conditions they have faced for generations, is likely to be spurious.

Black separatism has been twice rejected by Americans of all ethnicities, but white separatism, masquerading as cultural pluralism, is now claiming acceptance by the same group that rejected black separatism. The why of these actions is not very clear. Social scientists have been unable to produce objective conclusions about any social phenomenon of wide significance because their values and ideology are confused with the selection and manipulation of data. They are part of the very thing they study. It is therefore quite critical that the ideology of the social scientists, or any scientist, for that matter, be examined along with the acceptance of his/her facts or conclusions. In the instant argument over pluralism, it is difficult to separate how one feels, or what one wishes for America, from the selected facts themselves. To the serious reader, it should be clear that my personal bias is in the direction of the "oneness" of America. For me to claim that I now favor or ever favored, or even saw merit in, separatism and pluralism, would be dishonest. It is my firm belief that America's greatness has lain in her insistence on nonrecognition of any cultural, religious, ethnic, or racial group, except for the express purpose of bringing them into greater citizenship.

But social scientists have been able to couch their ideology in the rhetoric of objectivity while seizing upon nonobjective data to consolidate their arguments. Head-scratching and foot-shuffling by blacks in the presence of whites in the Old South were interpreted as caste etiquette by scholars who believed in caste.[11] Black scholars who opposed the caste position could hardly get published to make their opposition known. Likewise it was easier to gain publication for support of the general position of black inferiority than for support of one suggesting equality with or assimilation into the larger American family.[12] Whether it was planned or not, there seemed to be considerable agreement among scholars in the social sciences that blacks were a caste.

Today there is an emerging uniformity concerning the logic and prevalence of cultural pluralism in America. The source of these similarities seem located in the tendencies of social scientists to become directed in their studies and writings by powers greater than themselves. Their findings become set in place and resist displacement or refutation even when they are clearly in error. The more books and articles written, the more the findings are footnoted. After some time it is incorporated into the thoughts of the constituency—students and the reading public—that these findings are both objectively valid and representative of the general feelings of the public. The incorrect, by a process of common interpretation and continuous presentation has become viewed as correct.

The pluralist position is most strongly supported by scholars who believe it validly represents a program for the country at large. It is rejected just as vehemently by those who feel it is detrimental to the country. Data supportive of either position are selective, and arguments and data not supportive of a desired position are cast aside. But data are seldom the basis for belief in either the pluralist or the assimilationist position. Much is a matter of personal belief, which is never independent of the extent to which one has been socialized or manipulated by the media. Presently the believers in pluralism have been able to monopolize the media and are able to make many believe in the plausibility of their program.

Politically, concessions are made to both the pluralists and the assimilationists. Pluralists are allowed a few grants and resources to propagandize their viewpoints at conferences, in books, and elsewhere. At the same time the antipluralists are encouraged to continue their fight to lift barriers to the inclusion of more people into the economy and culture on a nonethnic basis. The financing of debates and programs, separatist and integrationist, comes from the same general sources: the decision-making quasi-governmental bodies and the foundations. This will continue until there is clear resolution of the issue to the extent that heavy policy can be implemented in favor of one or another of the philosophies. Governmental bodies and policymakers will have taken their cues from social scientists. Social scientists will have provided the foundations for the rhetoricians of separatism and assimilationism. All will claim to have spoken with the grass roots to obtain a feel for what the people want.

Neither a pure assimilationist nor a pure separatist president has ever occupied the White House. Each president, from George Washington forward, has sensed it to be politically inexpedient to become too solidly entrenched in either of these camps. Each has looked for a program which would placate those constituencies perceived as affecting presidential futures. For years, of course, ideas such as "strict constructionism" allowed presidents to shirk their responsibility to support the rights of all citizens, by allowing states greater power than the federal government. But from around the period of World War 1, each president has sensed the developing "twoness" of America, and most have asked the citizens to ignore differences and work for the common good.

Social scientists have been reluctant to draw conclusions from their studies which will not be politically or socially acceptable. Findings need not be accepted by all but by what are perceived as important segments of society. Fear of losing the respect of peers and being disqualified from consideration for future grants, awards, or foundation support strongly control many social scientists. At a time when government is supporting policies of pluralism, assimilationists will not be considered as having worthwhile plans for social change. If assimilationists come to power, the separatists will have a hard time surviving.

At present there is the danger of social scientists failing to warn the country that it becomes uncontrollably weak when fragmented into pluralistic and separate enclaves. Ethnic division is like the biological process of mitosis. Each group divides at its first opportunity and continues to do so until it becomes too weak and enervated to divide further. Then it dies. The fissuring of America has occurred along racial lines but will not stop there. Few anticipate that more than one fracture is in the offing. Societies which fracture continue to do so until they crumble into a thousand little pieces. Fracturing means eventual disintegration, for it is a process of irreversible decay. Those countries which are badly fractured seem to be in more advanced stages of decay than those resisting it more strongly. (We cannot offer at this time a formal scale of the decay of countries, but there are some much weaker than others. The weak ones seem most fractured. A good example is India, which attempts to solve internal inequalities by division and catering to the politics of pluralism.)

Long before formal social science made its entry into the American scene, the country had become conceptually divided into North and South. The tools of social science were used to create the mentality that there were two Americas, each with different policies, citizen rights, and responsibilities. Writers tried to isolate northern and southern mentalities, and none was more successful than Harriet Beecher Stowe who portrayed these mentalities vividly in *Uncle Tom's Cabin.*

After the Civil War conceptual division continued. The idea emerged that northerners were different from southerners because of differences in speech. And within these broad categories internal groups differed from each other—northern whites differed from southern whites and northern white Protestants differed from southern white Protestants until a thousand differences were noted. Regionalism seemed logical to men like Howard Odum who could not envision a unified America. Not being able to do so prevented their seriously criticizing American pluralism and separatism.

The breaking of the country into two racial camps was nerve-wracking enough; now it threatens to fragment into many more pluralistic and separate enclaves. For, seeing that there was some support for pluralism by ethnic peoples, social scientists begin to interpret pluralism favorably. Pluralists establish themselves unobtrusively at first. Analyses by social scientists who are pluralists initially show that the ethnic group seeking to withdraw into its own culture is simply trying to rediscover itself and its own past. Its concentration upon itself, to the exclusion of others, is not only applauded but is encouraged, for it is felt that strength resides in differences.

Preoccupation with the black problem has prevented social scientists from fully understanding the significance of other ethnic group separatism. These groups and their actions have not been thoroughly analyzed and dissected as have blacks. The conclusion seems plausible that white ethnic separatism is somehow more natural, more acceptable, than black separatism. Accordingly, if white ethnics ghettoize, their culture is said to be enhanced, for it is venerable and authentic. The pathologies of ghettoization are minimized or unrealized as they hide under the euphoria of separatism. If blacks ghettoize, their condition is cause for national alarm, for all can see the negative consequences of such a program. Ironically, now, two pathologies are explained, so that one is favorable and the other unfavorable. It is our belief that as social science begins to scrutinize carefully the new ethnicity, the new pluralism, it will conclude it is as weak theoretically and practically as black separatism always has been.

Academia is no more unified in its interpretation of social phenomena than any other group. Some disputes, to be sure, are results of honest differences in interpretation of data. In other cases, academic people may try to direct the ideology and practice of a country, or some part of it, by rendering questionable interpretations of data or reaching conclusions in agreement with their social biases. A generation ago social scientists were caught in a political atmosphere which looked toward the assimilation of white ethnic groups, but they were practically forced to support the unequal status of blacks. It was very much like the situation during slavery when those who opposed slavery were considered deviant and dangerous. Abolitionists were sometimes treated as different species of white people, and many suffered socially and economically as a result. Sigmund Livingston noted in 1946 that some academics fabricated data and conclusions to make their viewpoints acceptable.[13] Many instances of dishonesty may be found among academic people where their findings have important social consequences. Biases are often deep-seated and become confused with a logic of correctness. What we hope for is conditioned by our training, which naturally affects and determines our biases.

Data alone will not resolve the argument of evolution versus biblical creation, for biases are rigidly set in one direction or the other. Likewise the idea of America as a pluralist or assimilationist country can be understood best in terms of the biases developed, maintained, or changed which result from our socialization. People conditioned to inequality think in terms of pluralism, while equality-minded ones cannot conceive of society productively structured in any other way.

The ideology of pluralism is found in many of the major works of the social science tradition. We need only mention at this point some of the better known writers in order to substantiate our contention. W. G. Sumner was a pluralist who openly favored elitism. L. F. Ward thought that pluralism was a function of evolution and that a certain amount of social planning was necessary to compensate for the poor evolutionary position of some mistreated groups. Today the greatest support for the pluralist position is found in conservative academics, the academics of class, caste, and biological inequality.[14] Social scientists have often rebelled against the teachings of their forebears, for they have suspected them of using ideology as a substitute for conclusions drawn from data. In the 1960s a vocal minority of liberally trained scholars objected to any plan which would resegregate America, though they were unsure that they wanted full equality for blacks. They were drowned out by the ideologues of the right, whose arguments and political influence convinced the people to retreat from the thrust toward equality and move backward into the politics of pluralism.

10

POLITICAL AND CULTURAL PLURALISM
COMPARED

In order to better understand the relationship between political and cultural pluralism, it is necessary to draw upon the experiences of some countries where both exist. Since current emphasis is heavily on the pluralisms of Africa, many of the references will be to those countries. Afterwards I argue that cultural and political pluralism rest on the same premises in their attitudes toward social interaction.

Scholars such as J. S. Furnivall[1] observed pluralism in India and the Indies in the 1940s and felt it might be applicable to America. Anthropologists probably used the term earliest, and usually applied it to cultures and groups with widely different lifeways. Later, political scientists used it to refer to diverse groups of some noticeable homogeneity within a restricted geographical area. Homogeneity was used as the basis of political power, in that disparate groups voted together as a bloc. Still later, sociologists began to use the term pluralism, arguing that groups wanted to preserve their likenesses, for those common features, values, and beliefs are the bases for feelings of pride, self-worth, and mental health.

After all these disciplines made their feelings toward pluralism known (and we believe we are justified in calling them feelings, since they are not derived from data or logic), the idea of pluralism began to sweep America as an intellectual movement. Much of the inspiration for this sweep was based upon government or foundation sponsored studies of relatively obscure African or Third World ethnic groups formerly known as tribes. Most of the studies were done in the 1960s when these territories were gaining their independence. However, their failure to become integrated nations overnight was now attributed to tribalism. Tribes inhibited political growth, trade, and cooperation with European or other Western powers. Tribalism and national growth were soon seen as incompatible. Men who could rise above their tribal connections and unite the people into larger and more functional polities were supported for elective office. In Ghana Kwame Nkrumah talked about an Africa united, where tribe would mean little, where an African would simply be a person integrated into the system of prosperity. After a few years Nkrumah was overthrown.[2] In the Congo Patrice Lumumba tried to do the same and was killed.[3] The story was much the same in Zanzibar, where cultural pluralism led to political pluralism, then to economic pluralism, and finally to racial inequality. John Okello's revolt in 1964 overthrew the Arabs, downgraded the Indians, and installed indigenous Africans in positions of leadership.[4]

On the mainland Jomo Kenyatta was chosen as leader of multi-ethnic Kenya. Until his death he worked to eliminate tribalism and racism.[5] Milton Obote of Uganda abolished the traditional kingdoms in the mid-1960s, trying to pave the way for a prosperous Uganda without the detriments of tribalism.[6] A revolution was required to oust Haile Selassie from his feudal hold on Ethiopia, where he had exploited ethnic and religious divisions to the economic advantage of his own Amhara group and himself.[7] He did this with the assistance of Western powers, for more than forty years.

South Africa is probably the most notorious of the tribes-makers with its program of Bantustans and general apartheid.[8] Little imagination is required to understand who is profiting from ethnic pluralism in that lovely land of such ugly social life.

A most recent case of the instability of the politics of cultural and ethnic pluralism is seen in the case of Liberia. For 120 years a handful of ex-American slave descendant families ruled Liberia. They became very prosperous while the general constituency stagnated in poverty. The immigrants used their literacy and connections with America to manage the affairs of America and other countries in Liberia. But the Americo-Liberians were overthrown in a coup in the spring of 1980. Their lifestyles and values differ from the indigenous Liberians, whose hatred for them had simmered for decades.

Although African and other Third World leaders have struggled to eradicate the parochialisms of pluralistic societies, scholars from the West are busy arguing that Africans are clamoring to understand and protect their territory by getting back to their roots. Parochialism, tribalism, and nationalism have all become fused into an ideology of separatism. And now Miss Colson can state that a group as relatively isolated and dependent as the Tonga of Zambia have become very self-centered and are no longer as tolerant of strangers as they were in the past.[9] Africans are now subtly encouraged to utilize or cultivate their ethnic or tribal identities, for these are based on the natural and deep-seated affinities of kinship. Western primordialists and pluralists are supplying some theoretical support for this emphasis.[10]

Sociologists may have drawn their ideas on cultural pluralism from theories of political pluralism. Reactions to ruling elite models of society, models popularized in the works of such scholars as Floyd Hunter, Lloyd Warner, Robert and Helen Lynd, and others, led to the popularization of pluralistic models wherein groups of actors have differential power in the political system. Robert Dahl and Charles E. Lindblom claim that bargaining can exist best under social pluralism. Here is a mixture of goal agreement, conflict, and interdependence. Social pluralism is a diversity of social organizations with a large measure of autonomy with respect to one another. Social pluralism is seen as a base for political pluralism. Pluralism develops a complex distribution of control. Dahl and Lindblom believe the extent of pluralism is inversely related to elitism, or that the extent of bargaining is inversely related to the amount of hierarchy.[11]

Cultural pluralism often corresponds to political pluralism. Yet it is not clear why there should be an assertion of cultural pluralism when what may be meant is political pluralism. According to the pluralistic viewpoint in politics, different groups bargain, compete, and conflict to control the desirable values of society. The divergent groups may not represent different cultures; they are merely seeking power to control resources beneficial to themselves. Membership changes in politically pluralistic groups for they are not necessarily culturally different. They believe the same things are valuable, which causes the conflict. The values in dispute are believed to be in too short supply to be distributed equitably.

Genuinely pluralistic societies, i.e., culturally pluralistic societies, are not characterized by conflict, for the different cultures do not share value systems. Pastoral nomads and sedentary agriculturalists lived in East Africa for generations without significant conflict. Pastoralists might raid other cattlekeepers, but were very little interested in the farmers. Each had little knowledge of, and some contempt for, the other. They shared very few institutions. Through colonialism they were forced to share some values—work, the wearing of clothes, access to European beer, and compulsory payment of taxes, for example. The caste system in India generated little conflict so long as members of different castes did not compete for common values. In our own society, the very religious Amish and Mennonites do not conflict with those of more conventional religions, for their lifeways and values are quite different.

When groups share values, conflict erupts over access when those values are perceived as scarce. Conflict was inevitable between American settlers and Indians once they both accepted land as a value in limited supply. Their common valuation of land was an important step in placing them in similar cultural spheres. Slavery and black oppression in America were/ are systems of high conflict, for whites and blacks from the earliest times have operated out of the same value system. Freedom, equality, and equal aceess to the good things of America evidently were defined as scarce, and subordinate groups were unwilling to concede their scarcity and submit to unequal distribution.

Cultural pluralism and political pluralism are closely related. It is not merely a matter of which came first. They are conceptually and actually intertwined and can neither be adequately described nor explained separately. There are some slight cultural differences between groups of Americans, but the more they associate the more similar their cultures become. Nonassociation promotes cultural differences. Pluralism is fundamentally a consequence of nonassociation of groups. If political factors prevent close group and personal interaction, it is inevitable that differences will arise which, over time, will become politically significant. This elementary lesson has long been understood by most American leaders. To promote harmony one promotes association: to foster hatred one promotes nonassociation.

Nowhere do we find the magnitude of differences separating Americans that exist in even small countries of Europe or the countries of the Third World. Wherever cultural pluralism has existed, some minority groups have been forced to fight for political involvement and representation, for pluralism has been a signal to the dominant group to control the political spectrum while preserving cultural heterogeneity. The native Americans were probably the very first to be deprived of their civil rights under the thrust of cultural pluralism which rapidly combined with political pluralism. Their political subjugation was assured once it was evident they could not become full participants in Anglo or European culture while having no means to resist.

In early and adolescent America no formula could be found to assure culturally different groups adequate representation. The most different, such as the Indians and some religious groups, were practically excluded from political processes, and any political expression on their part was accomplished through white representatives.

While free black Americans were confined to plantations, they did not have direct representation in the halls of government. They gave up their vote in exchange for a shack and an opportunity to make a share-crop which placed them each year further in the "hole." Their representatives were persons who were uninterested in them and unfamiliar with their needs. Many Old South politicians campaigned on platforms of bigotry with definite intentions of detaining the progress of the blacks. Is there any reason to believe that ethnic politicians will do any different?

Under pluralism the ethnic group must give up its direct participation in the political and electoral processes in favor of some official, ethnic or otherwise, who purports to represent them. The reality of their poverty and limited mobility curbs the effectiveness of those who serve as their representatives. In terms of politics, the local ethnic hierarchy is so short that what power there is tends to concentrate in the hands of ward bosses who may become quite dictatorial in their domination of local ethnic areas. With communities divided up ethnically, minorities will be too weak to exert influence over any institutions except those directly concerned with their neighborhood life. The general political structure may say: "To control the Poles, see Symanski. Pay off Krueger and he'll handle the ethnic Germans. Chavez will take care of the Chicanos and Ramon the Spics. Of course 'Daddy King' will hold the blacks in place." Transfer of power from the people to the "boss," whether on the Old South plantation or on the new inner city ethnic plantation, is the very likely outcome of trying to convert ethnic constituencies to political parties. And the ethnic group must become a party if it intends to play a role in the control and management of its own or larger resources.

Political pluralism and cultural pluralism are alike in that they both require individuals to subordinate their desires to some higher entity such as the party or the ethnic group. There are many differences in any culture, and pluralists try to capitalize upon them. Political pluralism means fragmentation of the groups into numerous smaller ones with limited issues as their focus. Pluralistic groups are not interested in the same goals, and political pluralism loses its meaning in such a society. In foreign countries with centuries of cultural pluralism, political pluralism develops and causes those in power to show limited interest in the improvement of ethnic groups other than their own. India comes readily to mind where many groups were mistreated politically because they were perceived as culturally different. In Iran Farsi leaders may not be interested in the welfare of ethnic Russians living within their borders even though they are citizens of Iran. In the American Southwest Navaho children do not get a better education so long as their parents insist upon their remaining ethnic Navahos. Navahos are not perceived as basically different culturally from other Nevadans, the few peculiarities of the tribe notwithstanding. A Navaho background carries no more social weight than an English, German, or Italian one in a society with assimilation as its basic philosophy. Defining an ethnic or cultural group out of the general American cultural spectrum could lead to serious political neglect of the negatively defined group.

Conventional approaches to political pluralism claim it is an argument against political hierarchy, against domination by a few powerful figures at high levels of the political pyramid. In American politics, institutions are fairly well-balanced in terms of power. But a diffusion of power at top levels does not mean that individuals lower in the hierarchy are necessarily better off. The pluralism is at the top of the pyramid where powerful men have managed to gain control of vital institutional sectors. In order to consolidate control of an institutional sphere, that sphere must act as a bloc. Bloc voting can only lead to limited gains and then mainly in terms of the needs of the bloc. Persons in power but not of a given ethnic bloc may have no responsibility for or interest in those outside the bloc.

If there is great differentiation at the bottom of the pyramid, the separate blocs will be too small in number to wield many votes. Their influence will become localized and transferred to local leaders for representation. Their positions could not change greatly, for there would be no way to bring power to bear, because of their numerical weakness. Thus the price the ethnic group pays for playing the politics of ethnicity is a heavy one. To preserve its difference, the ethnic group must be satisfied with less than what it would receive as a member of a greater political constituency.

Cultural pluralism in America seems to be a euphemism for the preservation of old style, lower class, white ethnic ghettos. These areas are made up of people who never really tested American society to see how far their freedom extends. As H. L. Mencken observed in the 1920s, they were beaten down and driven from the Old World and were grateful for whatever they got in the New. Their horizons seldom extended beyond their ghetto walls, which they never understood were prisons.[12]

Politically, cultural pluralism is seen as a way of maintaining very tenuous social advantages while restricting the movement of those with whom elite groups do not wish to compete. The white ethnics in America were previously very hostile toward each other and perhaps still are today. The ethnics are joining Anglo society and adopting its culture more frequently than they are becoming ethnically intercultural. Evidence is scanty that white ethnics are willing to get along with each other in the U.S. They certainly have not done so in Canada, Spain, Ireland, eastern Europe, Russia, Israel, or South Africa. If anything, white American ethnics have gotten along better inside or on the borders of the black ghetto than they have within all-white communities where their ethnicity was not predominant.

The political consequences of cultural pluralism are obscured unless subjected to close analysis. Group theory suggests that the larger the number of persons comprising a group the greater the likelihood of its fragmenting into many smaller groups. That this is likely is seen by application of the very simple formula for permutations, $N(N-1)/2$, where N is the size of the group. With a group of two there can be only one faction, while with a group of six persons there can be as many as fifteen factions of two persons each. If the nation is taken as the unit of analysis and its factions counted, they could very quickly run into the hundreds. Factionalism could become so endemic that stern measures might be required to contain it toward some common norm.

Fascism is strong central control of all essential institutions. It permits no criticism of or deviation from its plan and policies. Fascism is not a representative form of government, for its leadership is not fairly elected. Nonelected leadership, by definition, must represent a faction or fraction of the total constituency since it is not representative of all. Fascism and factionalism are thereby rather close together in concept and practice. Government which fails to be representative tends toward fascism, and instability is inherent in this form.

A society characterized by significant pluralism must veer toward fascism, for there must be a strong central government to control the competing demands of the pluralistic groups. Such a government must utilize an authoritarian leader who coerces people into following his line of reasoning. Russia was forced into fascism after the revolution of 1917 when the only way to control more than one hundred competing nationality groups was by the coercion of communist dictatorship. Germany fell into the fascistic mold with the rise of Adolf Hitler, who sought to reduce pluralism by drastic means. Italy was characterized by great pluralism in the late 1930s and drifted into fascism.

America is drifting in the same direction. With many groups calling for ethnic pluralism, the way is open for the emergence of a strong central government to make sure each group is protected. Unfortunately, the protection of one group is interpreted as favoritism by another as seen in such cases as *Bakke*[13] and other affirmative action suits. Are American Indians being unduly favored when they are allowed access to millions of acres of land, virtually unpopulated, while millions of people are trapped in inner city slums without room for expansion or opportunities for decent standards of living or self-respect? Can the numerous Anglos fairly impose English on immigrants who feel comfortable with French,

Yiddish, Hindu, or Spanish? The option which must be followed with ethnic pluralism is governmental control.

Professional pluralists, many of whom are academics, understand that unless there is agreement on certain major values toward which all strive, there will be, most probably, little alternative but to sacrifice freedom for forced harmony by governmental control.

In a sense, pluralism is a variety of the old and familiar program of divide and conquer. While groups conflict over space, turf, and minor values, centrists work to entrench themselves in power at group expense. Fascism thrives where there is great fragmentation of a nation into incompatible groups with disunity as their central characteristic.

11

THE ROLE OF THE SCHOOL
IN PLURALISTIC TEACHING

The schools are on the front lines of any conflict such as that between ethnic pluralism and social integration. This is because the institution of formal education affects so many millions of young people for such a long time. Thoroughly committed ethnic people insist upon schools which they can control. By this means they control to a greater extent the values their children acquire.

It is only recently that various white ethnic groups have begun to insist upon respect for their values in the schools. They have had access to the same education as Anglo children and therefore could not claim the schooling of their children was substandard. Ordinarily, public funds have been available to finance education only if instruction was mainly in English. Groups wishing to supplement this instruction had to do so from private funds. Supplemental ethnic language and cultural programs were carried out after school, on Saturdays, at retreats, and occasionally in homes. Such programs had a very hard time succeeding because those attending were stigmatized. These children wanted to be involved in the activities of all other children and saw little need to have supplemental training in cultures they did not understand. The ethnic ways of parents have been an embarrassment to children, whose sentiments are always more assimilationist than pluralist.

The failure of school districts to fund ethnic language programs, except as a means of facilitating the learning of English, was interpreted by the ethnic peoples as indicating that their cultures were not held in high esteem. But the simple fact is that the children would be forced to learn English in order to participate more completely in the economic system once they reached adulthood. Only at the lowest levels of common labor was failure to understand English not a handicap.

Ethnic groups did not openly advocate separate schools for their children, but some did ask that their children be taught in their own language. Spanish-speaking populations, for example, have demanded bilingual programs—programs which would maintain the legitimacy of Spanish, the language of the home and the culture.[1] The thrust of ethnic groups toward compelling school districts to provide instruction in the language of the children attending the schools reached the U.S. Supreme Court in *Lau* v. *Nichols* (1974).[2] A few years later a Detroit judge ruled that the black ghetto dialect was not an inappropriate medium of instruction for inner city students and ordered the city schools to train teachers in this dialect.[3]

Separate language programs are probably the forerunners of separate schools. Soon more multi-ethnic education is required, ostensibly for the purpose of bringing groups together. The practical effect has been to pull them apart. On a national level, all the programs of cultural appreciation have not produced more harmonious schools or communities, but have fragmented them further. Inner city schools are becoming black and Hispanic and suburban schools increasingly white.

De facto segregation produced racially separate schools before they were declared illegal under the *Brown* decision. But white ethnics did not feel the full brunt of segregation since their children were mixed in with Anglo children and were involved in learning English. Their mixing was not so psychologically damaging to white ethnic children, for they had internalized the notion that they could not be considered real Americans unless they spoke unbroken English. They wanted to learn English as much as their teachers wanted them to. There were almost no rewards, and there may have been actual handicaps imposed for remaining too ethnic in the public schools.

White ethnic children were not as interesting to the other children as darker-skinned children from other cultures. Czechs, Poles, and Jews were not seen as people representing authentically different and interesting cultures, while Oriental, Hispanic, and black children were. The more mixed a child's background, the more interesting he was to the other children. Few ethnic children of European background could compete as objects of interest with an Oriental-looking, Spanish-speaking child who was black.

Following the *Brown* decision, schools came under some pressure to become pluralistic. In addition to being expected to teach in the language of the children in attendance, they were required to use textbooks which cast ethnic groups in a more favorable light. Administrative, teaching, and custodial staffs were expected to mirror the ethnic makeup of the communities and students. The concern with development of school staffs that are pluralistic has encouraged "quota systems" for various ethnic groups. The schools since the *Brown* decision have had no official ideology of pluralism or separatism. Even when the main problem involved the segregation of blacks, segregation was not the prevailing ideology. It was only through a long and continuous process that pluralistic ideology began to take hold. But only in the most retrogressive section of the country, the South, was this ideology allowed to stand virtually unchallenged. Even there the complicity of the courts was required to support the ideology and practice of separatism. Pluralistic ideology masqueraded under the illegal custom of separation of students by race.

The forces of racism did not accept the equality of American citizens and sought to restore separatism by erecting an ideology in support of it. For years after school desegregation was ordered by the courts, school districts used a variety of strategies to keep the schools segregated— voucher plans, freedom of choice, antibusing drives, intimidation of minority students, use of remedial programs to disqualify undesirable students from receiving instruction, the use of teacher competency tests, more for the purpose of reducing the number of minority group teachers than for assuring that all teachers are competent. Not to be forgotten, of course, are the cries for neighborhood schools and the academy movement, both of which are believed to have as their purpose the racial separation of school children.

As long as the fight over segregated schools was being waged between blacks and whites, it could be considered nonideological and racial. Scholars had not succeeded in proving that pluralistic separation was anything other than old-fashioned racial segregation. But then blacks complained about losing their cultural heritage in the process of desegregating the schools and insisted on having their heritage recognized in their new school environment. Anticipating that there would be an upsurge in ethnic interest in the schools, HEW began the Ethnic Heritage Studies Program of the Elementary and Secondary Education Act of 1965, under Title IX. As amended, this title stated:

The Ethnic Heritage Studies Program seeks to develop intercultural understanding within our culturally pluralistic society. More specifically, the aims of the programs are to help students learn more about the nature and role of ethnicity in their own lives and in the lives of others and to promote effective interactions among members of various ethnic groups in the United States.[4]

It was no doubt this title expressed a clear ideological commitment of the government to cultural and ethnic pluralism. The schools were to be the major vehicle for the recognition and realization of America as a culturally pluralistic society. Much money was spent in the schools to promote a sense of ethnic pluralism. This support from government funding led some to adopt an ideology of pluralism for the general society. Few persons criticized the logic of cultural pluralism in schools, and the ideology drifted toward acceptance.

The school is the chief institution in which the battle for cultural pluralism will be waged. It processes millions of individuals yearly, and it is logical that much of the change in the general society will be brought about in connection with the schools. Control of the schools is crucial, for if an idea is to be implanted firmly in a great number of people, the schools are the place to begin. If the schools can be made pluralistic, the idea can more easily be consolidated in the larger society. From this come the strategies of showing either that (a) pluralistic schools are less desirable than homogeneous ones or (b) homogeneous schools are less desirable than pluralistic ones. The separatist will unhesitatingly engage in actions which are contradictory. It does not make any difference to the separatist that his child is enjoying a black school and learning more in it. He would gladly sentence his child to attend a school he hates in order to preserve his own prejudices. We all have seen people forgo mobility rather than move into positions requiring they take orders from individuals they considered lower than themselves. Separatism is not merely an attitude; it must be translated into action, and these actions are often contradictory and nonproductive. Separatism quickly moves from an ideology to a status—a religion to be defended at all costs. Use of academics to consolidate this defense is not far-fetched. Indeed Christopher Jencks has claimed that types of schools make little difference in the performance of children on tests of academic achievement.[5]

For some years emphasis was on the poor quality of the inner city schools and the high quality of suburban ones. Inner city parents wanted the most competitive education for their children and accepted busing as a step toward that end. The suburbs reacted and used various delaying tactics to forestall the arrival of inner city youth. When these schemes failed, they fell back on the strategy of making the school uncomfortable for children of any ethnicity whose numbers were substantial and whose status was unusually low. Intimidation was thinly disguised until police were placed in some corridors to hold down conflicts. Of course, white children bused to black schools frequently felt they were being harassed by blacks. There is probably a relationship between a feeling of harassment and its actual existence. For example, a Klansman would feel he is being threatened more by the fact of his child's busing than would an integrationist who sees busing as a golden opportunity for children to grow up in harmony. But today the suburban schools are having the same problems as inner city schools. They are places where drugs and violence are becoming rather common, and the scores indicating competence in academic subjects are falling. As the inner city school was downgraded to ghetto status, so is the suburban school being downgraded.

To counter the trend toward busing some are saying that the suburban schools are no good; that children are receiving no better education than is being provided in inner city schools. The center city parents will keep their children in the neighborhood schools, leaving the suburban schools substantially free of blacks. The integrationists may continue to bus their children into the black ghettos since they are more concerned with race-mixing than with the education of their children. The general outcome will be the relative status quo of unmixed schools, this time encouraged by the spate of books and reports showing how poor the suburban schools are.

On college campuses black students, following the King riots, began their disengagement from whites. Their frequent and nonnegotiable demands called for separate dormitories, classes taught by black faculty members chosen by the students, more courses relevant to the black experience, and more emphasis on black culture. College officials often met these demands. Other ethnic students followed the lead of blacks and formed their own societies and area study sections. By 1978 the campuses of America could be described as moving toward greater polarization and separation by race and ethnicity.[6]

The ideology of pluralism serves to defeat the concept of education as a broadening and liberalizing influence, for now students are avoiding each other if they are of different race or ethnicity. By doing so they fail to learn to appreciate the lifeways of others. Pluralism is becoming institutionalized in the colleges, with bureaucracy and positions created purely for the benefit of minority group students. Nearly every college has a minority affairs officer who elaborates programs and positions which have the practical effect of catering to distinct ethnic clienteles.

Educational philosophy has always been more important than educational practice, for philosophy gives direction and meaning to practice. A practice is more easily clarified if its underlying philosophy is known. It has never been a widely accepted philosophy that America would be a "nation of nations," even though it has been recognized that some persons would prefer if it were. The schools therefore were never to reflect the nationalisms of immigrant peoples who failed to identify with America. Black Americans were, of course, the most potentially nationalistic. Under the influence of remnants of Garveyism, Muslim separatist ideology, and academic definitions of black ghettos as internal colonies, black youth began to disdain the educational system as one which was hypocritical and unwilling to speak to the needs of the depressed community. Many youths became so alienated from the educational system that their competence in academic skills dropped sharply. Jensenism[7] claimed that the average tested differences separating blacks from whites were genetically determined. Environmentalists held to the notion that the differences were due to factors such as poor teaching, poor student motivation, and indirect efforts to undermine the faith of the student in any relationship between academic achievement and economic success. Philosophically, Jensenism was a strategy to promote the pluralism of the country by identifying a group which would be unable to participate fully in its economic and social life because of inferior genetic abilities. Conflict erupted in the schools when minority groups failed to accept the labels of inferiority pinned on them by academics.

Understanding the social implications of the philosophy of Jensenism, other ethnic groups sought to establish themselves between the whites and the blacks. Though they had conceded the top of the socioeconomic ladder to the Anglos, they would surely not fall to the bottom of it. For them a program of pluralism would remove the blacks and Anglos as competitors and they would fall into niches similar to the ones they maintained in their former countries. Pluralism would lower the level of frustration caused by the relative deprivation they would experience from their unsuccessful competition with the Anglos.

But both ethnics and blacks were unable to gain jobs as the economy tumbled and their bitterness and hostility festered. Educational specialists identified their problems as originating in poor earlier schooling and recommended compensatory and remedial programs. Most of these programs were integrative, for they sought to correct the weaknesses of the students. Once rehabilitated, the students would enter the economic system as full-fledged members with the usual loyalties to the system.

Pluralism on the campus has been encouraged by the international crisis over oil. Students from the oil producing nations (OPEC) and those from oil-dependent ones are now ideological enemies. Both groups cluster together much more than they did a decade ago. The new wealth of the OPEC students places them in higher economic brackets than American students. The social status of the students is reversed. Gas price hikes create hostility on the campuses between OPEC students and American students. Of course, the U.S. hostage crisis in Iran has done little to foster feelings of friendship between American and Near Eastern students. Third World students align with OPEC students in order to register their disaffection with U.S. policies abroad.

The outcome of all this is that foreign and American students have little to say to each other, in class or out. Campuses are becoming fragmented into nationalistic ghettos as groups of students seek ways of avoiding contact with those not of their ethnic or political persuasion. Student unions can now be studied ecologically as students from different countries and political blocs stake out space and practically monopolize it for their own use.

Even domestic students are less willing to interact with those different from themselves in race or slightly different in culture. Each group elaborates its own activities with few plans for the inclusion of outsiders. And it is done with the help of advisors who are committed to pluralism. Instead of students exhibiting international and world cultural outlooks, they are showing greater conservatism and provincialism than at any other time in recent history.

The chief struggle over educational philosophies appears to be waged between the black and white constituents of the schools and colleges. But if other ethnic groups pursue pluralism it is practically certain that they will face the same problems as blacks. In the schools of either level of instruction, few teachers will wish to be identified permanently as minority group teachers. Status and rewards can hardly be expected to issue from the minority communities. Students, likewise, will find little that is positive in being reminded a thousand times daily that they are Jewish, Polish, Chicano, or black. If they cannot be accepted as regular members of the school, since nonacceptance means their ethnicity is not good, they will contemplate withdrawal to establish their own schools and educational programs. Colleges and other institutions will then need to be established to cater to those students who have progressed through ethnic lower schools and programs so that the gains made will not be eroded by reentry into a world where their ethnicity has little currency. In time, then, America will become ethnically divided like the countries of the rest of the world. The schools will have been large contributors to it.

There has been a change in the attitudes of scholars interested in the question of the education of different social groups. This change has come about because of a shift in political philosophy toward differences. Politically, Americans never allowed true cultural differences to exist within the country. It was not simply ethnocentrism which prevented other genuinely different cultures from becoming established; the very organization of the country was geared to respond to a single predominant cultural format. The system of government, schools, economics, sports, lifestyles, and nearly all else catered to a mass of people essentially within the same cultural mold. Mexican food can be cooked by almost anyone. All American main streets and suburbs and slums look pretty much alike. Middle class life among assimilated native Americans is no different in quality from that of the Anglo middle class, nor are there important differences in speech patterns or religious practices.

Scholars have accounted for the failure of groups to reach the main-stream on the basis of alienation and discrimination, and the two have never been completely separated. Groups of whites who proposed and tried new lifestyles during the 1960s were openly alienated from the system. Their frustrations were a reaction to their inability to reform the system and redirect it along channels they considered more humane. Their withdrawal into communes and drugs was a statement against materialism, though many of those withdrawing had been privileged all their lives. They were more frustrated because the poor people, blacks and ethnic whites, did not follow them and continued toward the goals of the past. Poor blacks still wanted Cadillacs, and ethnic whites wanted homes in the suburbs with all the trappings of materialism.

Since the ideology of pluralism was accepted and promoted by government, scholars began to believe it was correct and started to tailor academic interpretations to conform to political practice. What were considered curious differences have now advanced, through political and academic agreement, to the status of legitimate cultures not to be integrated into the mainstream, thereby adding to the fragmentation of the country.

12

CULTURAL PLURALISM
THE DEVELOPMENT OF AN IDEA AND A CONCEPT

What are the intellectual bases of cultural pluralism in American society? Why did it emerge in academic thought at the time it did, and what are its consequences for the society at large? Although there is evidence that pluralism as an idea is found in a variety of disciplines, my intention is to concentrate on the idea as it exists and has developed in sociology.

In early human society differences within and between groups, were not socially important. Man was part of the natural order; size, coloration, and sex, had no social significance. With the development of language and thinking, distinctions began to be made between men, but there is no evidence that this was of anything but rudimentary social importance. Centuries passed after the civilization of man before he was divided into important social categories.

Anthropologists were among the first of modern scholars to study group differences systematically. They tried to understand them as they functioned within their own cultural contexts. Evolutionists, though, tried to arrange cultures on a scale of development, with simple people at the bottom and western Europeans at the top. They failed to convince their readers that men differed significantly because of their separate genetic histories.

By the time American scholars seriously entered the field of group study, they could draw upon European theory, which by the mid-nineteenth century was placing emphasis on social categories. Race was used to classify large groups in America. Marginal peoples had to fit into black or white categories.[1] Blacks and whites lived in segregated societies but did not evolve different cultures. The two societies were not allowed to interact on an equal basis and any association between them was dealt with harshly. Separation by race was thorough until the 1950s but never 100 percent.

Immigrants, nearly all from Europe, were not seen as ethnic, for there was no niche for ethnic people in America. They were viewed as white people from different cultures who would vanish into the mainstream as soon as they were able. Until around the 1930s immigrants accumulated in the slums of the great cities. After the Old Immigration, cheap land was harder to acquire and city life was the only practical option. As new-comers became successful, or assimilated, they took up living in neighbor-hoods homogeneous mostly by class, not by nationality. The ideology of mobility and absorption into the mainstream required that success-ful people abandon their poorer ethnic neighborhoods.

There was a contest between immigrants and blacks for the poorest living space in the great cities after World War 1 as blacks began to vacate the plantations of the South for better economic opportunities. Ironically, the European immigrants and the blacks got along better than the blacks and the Anglos, who were protected by a high wall of racism and exclusive political power. The comparable poverty of urban immigrants from Europe and the incoming blacks threw them together in slums which had little character as proud ethnic neighborhoods.

Before the 1960s there was almost no academic interest in nonblack ethnicism and cultural pluralism in American scholarship. But in 1963 Moynihan and Glazer claimed to have rediscovered the persistence of ethnicity among blacks, Puerto Ricans, Irish, Italians, and Jews in New York City. Their book *Beyond the Melting Pot* is said to have stimulated an "ethnic renaissance."

Beyond the Melting Pot made hardly a stir upon publication, but after the Watts riots and the violence which wracked the country between 1965 and 1970, the government was forced to make a considerable number of concessions toward the equal citizenship of black people. Jobs opened up, neighborhoods were integrated, youths were trained in prestigious fields, corporations appointed blacks to their boards. Blacks made enough economic progress to make other groups believe they had the formula to success. They were gaining on certain categories of the white popu-lation, and the poorer of the whites began to complain of black pre-ference. These whites wanted to cash in on the magic of ethnicity and needed a philosophical basis from which to make their demands. Richard Nixon had given them an opening when he appealed to the silent majority in his 1972 campaign for reelection. His landslide victory signaled the cohesiveness of the non-Anglo whites, most of whom were close to poor, and a closing of the ranks against the blacks. It was tantamount to a restoration of a Bourbon aristocracy to power in the White House. White people would once again be in charge of the lawless minorities and black people seated at the back of the bus. As the different groups of whites looked around for justification for their new found political strength, they were pointed toward such works as *Beyond the Melting Pot* which contained the thesis of the strength of ethnicity in modern life. The ethnic renaissance could now begin.

Soon books began streaming off the presses in a veritable tide of ink, propagandizing the greatness of this or that ethnic group. In most of the large cities "ethnic communities" appeared which formerly were simply called slums. Each neighborhood, no matter how poor, claimed to be held together by history, race, and ritual; each trying to survive in the face of an impersonal government bent on destroying its venerable culture. Slum clearance was interpreted as the dispersal of their people to alien environments, placing them at the mercy of the snobbish Anglos, or adjacent to blacks or their close relatives the Hispanics, or Asians, whose lifeways and culture had no appeal.

Out of this leaderless, anomic, debilitating condition across the ethnic prophets, the Michael Novaks and the Andrew Greeleys, all admonishing the ethnics to abandon the belief that they would ever be accepted in America. They were told to make a life for themselves upon the bedrock of their culture; primordialism and ethnicism. They were reminded they never had much in common with blacks, but should use the blacks' tactics if that would help gain consideration by the government. And the cry went out: "Politicize your ethnicity; use it to your advantage!"

In book after book, and article after article, most published after 1973, we find some statement about the revival of ethnicity. Definitions of it include the by now familiar references to linguistic, national, and religious groups. Although the blacks were considered a racial group they were nearly always discussed as an ethnic group. There was no clear way of separating ethnicity, race, and culture. Ethnic pluralism and cultural pluralism became confused and were often used synonymously.

The term cultural pluralism has not always been found in American sociology textbooks. Before about the mid-1970s it probably was not in widespread use in any of the social sciences. But very close to it were such terms as "cultural relativity" and "cultural heterogeneity," which were found in many of the introductory textbooks. In order to get some idea of how the term cultural pluralism became incorporated in textbooks in general sociology, I inspected indexes containing the headings "culture," "cultural pluralism," and "pluralism." If reference to any of these terms was made, I examined the context and meaning in the specific pages indicated. The accompanying table summarizes these

USE OF TERM "CULTURAL PLURALISM" IN SOCIOLOGY TEXTS

YEAR	AUTHOR(S)	TITLE	NOT USED	USED
1921	R.E. Park and E.W. Burgess	Introduction to the Science of Sociology	X	
1934	K. Young	An Introductory Sociology	X	
1940	T. H. Robinson et al.	Men, Groups, and Community	X	
1946	R.T. LaPierre	Sociology	X	
1946	W. Ogburn and M.F. Nimkoff	Sociology	X	
1950	W. Ogburn and M.F. Nimkoff	Sociology, 2nd ed.	X	
1953	J. Biesanz and M. Biesanz	Modern Society	X	
1958	W. Ogburn and M.F. Nimkoff	Sociology, 3rd ed.	X	
1961	R.L. Sutherland, J. Woodward, and M.A. Maxwell	Introductory Sociology, 6th ed.	X	
1963	G.A. Lundberg, C. Schrag, and O.N. Larsen	Sociology, 3rd ed.		X
1963	A. Gouldner and H.P. Gouldner	Modern Sociology	X	
1964	R.E.L. Faris	Handbook of Modern Sociology	X	
1964	P.B. Horton and C.L. Hunt	Sociology, 2nd ed.	X	
1965	K. Young and R. Mack	Sociology and Social Life, 3rd ed.	X	
1965	J. W. Vander Zanden	Sociology: A Systematic Approach		X
1966	F.J. Woods	Introductory Sociology		X
1967	E. Chinoy	Society	X	
1968	A. Green	Sociology	X	
1968	J. Cuber	Sociology: A Synopsis of Principles		X
1969	M. Abrahamson	Sociology: An Introduction to Concepts, Methods, and Data	X	
1969	J. Biesanz and M. Biesanz	Introduction to Sociology		X
1971	T. Caplow	Elementary Sociology	X	

YEAR	AUTHOR(S)	TITLE	NOT USED	USED
1971	H. M. Hodges	*Conflict and Consensus: An Introduction to Sociology*, 2nd ed.	X	
1973	M. Tumin	*Patterns of Society*	X	
1973	M.L. Defleur, W. D'Antonio, and L.R. Defleur	*Sociology: Human Society*		X
1973	J. Douglas	*Introduction to Sociology*		X
1973	L. Broom and P. Selznick	*Sociology*, 5th ed.		X
1974	J. B. McKee	*Introduction to Sociology*, 2nd ed.		X
1975	W.J. Chambliss and T.E. Ryther	*Sociology: The Discipline and its Direction*		X
1975	D. Light, Jr., and S. Keller	*Sociology*		X
1977	I. Robertson	*Sociology*		X

findings by year, author(s), titles of text, and whether or not the term of cultural pluralism was used. Pluralism, in the textbooks, when not conceived as cultural pluralism, usually refers to political groups checking each other in a power dimension. The democratic model of power is analyzed in the writing of Robert Dahl[2] who believed power resided in a variety of groups with different issues foremost for them. The elitist model of power is discussed by C. W. Mills[3] who feels that power is centralized in interlocking national decision-makers referred to as *the power elite*. Generally, both of these concepts of pluralism, referring to power, were discussed in the texts.

The first observations of cultural pluralism were probably in reference to societies other than America. J. S. Furnivall, for example, was impressed by the extent of segregation in colonial society in Indonesia and Burma. There the Europeans formed the top of the social order, the Chinese and Indians the middle layer, and the indigenous people the bottom. "Each group holds its own religion, its own culture, its own ideas and ways. As individuals they meet, but only in the market place, in buying and selling."[4] M. G. Smith used the concept in 1953.[5] Later, in 1960, Smith noted that pluralism is correlated with inequality and stratification.[6]

Even though Lundberg, Schrag, and Larsen used the term "cultural pluralism" in their 1963 text, it was probably Milton Gordon, whose book *Assimilation in American Life* (1964) made the term relatively popular. The way the term is used after 1965 refers essentially to the way Gordon used it in his 1964 work. He considered it to mean diversity of ethnic and racial groups and their adjustment to each other in a limited time and space frame. But since reaching considerable use in general sociology texts, the term cultural pluralism has not been defined consistently.

Earl Babbie (*Society by Agreement,* 1977) envisions pluralism as a sociocultural situation in which cultural differences are perpetuated side by side in the same society, each culture being allowed to retain its distinct agreements. He also assumes that each subculture has a reasonably fair share of power in the society.

Perry and Perry believe (see *The Social Web,* 1979) pluralism stresses the desirability of each ethnic group's retaining its cultural distinctiveness, rather than being assimilated into the dominant culture. They claim that American blacks have a different culture from whites. While admitting the destruction of black culture during slavery, they contend that blacks developed a new culture, customs, and traditions which vary from those of the majority. The Perrys even hint that the speech of many blacks, although based on English, can be virtually unintelligible to other cultural groups, and perhaps intentionally so.

A neat definition of pluralism could be maintained if the complicating case of the blacks did not exist. Where groups have very similar cultures, as do blacks and Anglos and many European descendants who have adopted Anglo culture, no profound argument can be made for their pluralism. One must account for any differences in terms of limitations of opportunity which can be considered discrimination. Shifting from discrimination to free cultural choice placed the burden upon the depressed group to show why they should not be proud of their racial or separate cultural heritage.

There has been no clear demonstration of the cultural difference of blacks who have adopted the same values and standards of the rest of American society. In fact, the resistance of blacks to accepting a different classification from the majority Americans is seen in a few of the following examples:

1. Blacks have had to know white majority culture in order to earn their living in that culture since they have not had the economic means for self-support.

2. They have objected to different schooling on grounds that what was seen as different was determined by the courts (*Brown* decision) to be inferior education.

3. The adults of black society object to teachers allowing "Black English" to substitute for standard English. They know that while "Black English" may be colorful and expressive in the slums and isolated black communities, it is not helpful in the competition of modern society. Blacks have long realized that pluralism represents separation and inequality, and are not impressed by findings such as those of George Ritzer et al, who state: "The primary advocates of pluralism have been minority spokespersons. . . . Pluralism . . . implies recognition of cultural equality among ethnic groups, not the superiority of one. It accepts cultural homogeneity."[7]

Blacks have been the major spokespersons and litigants on the issue of equality. They have never argued that black culture be closed to any other group and they have pressed for inclusion in the American dream rather than exclusion. Seldom have they advocated a separate society, and those who have, have not experienced success. The "black is beautiful" phase of the struggle attempted to show America that blacks are part of the main culture and that the beauty of their contribution is obvious. It has not been suggested that broken homes, unemployment, illness, and poverty, all heavily represented in any catalogue of black life, are beautiful.

Ritzer et al equate cultural groups, ethnic groups, and power groups. If two groups which have different cultures have the same amount of power, or lack of it, then individuals can make their choice of the culture in which they wish to participate. Whites who want to engage in black culture would not be discouraged from doing so. Blacks preferring white culture would be encouraged in their choice. But Ritzer et al know there is no cultural equality in America, for they understand that separate culture, as used in America, means separation by race or ethnicity.

A most comprehensive treatise on the topic of cultural pluralism is Crawford Young's The Politics of Cultural Pluralism.[8] This book is a careful compilation of instances of former colonial cultures which continued to squabble among themselves when the colonialists disappeared. Young does not claim an integrative force in cultural pluralism, but shows just the opposite, that cultures are not appreciative of each other. He is clearly not interested in getting trapped into a position on American pluralism, for he understands that American pluralism is different from pluralism anywhere else in the world, if it exists at all. American pluralism is commercial and so far without deep cultural significance. All old Americans, no matter their original ethnicity, have about the same culture. Young admits the melting pot ideology went almost unchallenged into the 1960s, but he skirts the issue by ignoring the uniqueness of the

American case. The older cultures of the world were already steeped in internal cultural hatred long before America was born. Is it valid to compare old and new cultures when they were formed on very different premises?

Why the pluralistic idea took hold in sociology cannot be explained by the appearance of the term alone. Scholars before the 1960s understood that there were many different ethnic groups in America. Most knew that those immigrants most closely guarding their ethnic ties and failing to become widely involved in the larger culture remained the poorest. Nearly all were trying to scrap behavior and values which prohibited movement into the middle class. Pluralism was not seriously entertained by those ethnic groups which thought they could gain entry to the middle class. Few ethnics wilfully chose to remain segregated and distinct in ethnic communities. Nearly all white ethnics wanted to melt, and many did. Many changed their culture but could not change their poverty; almost none changed from poverty to affluence without changing their culture in the direction of the American middle class.

As can be seen from the evidence presented, cultural pluralism has moved toward becoming established as a concept in sociology. It is probably being established in other social science disciplines as well. Pluralism was barely represented in textbooks examined before 1963. Its use was intermittent until 1973, after which it began to appear regularly and gained philosophical sanction in the process. Along with this has been a tendency to portray indigenous cultural groups as incurably different. In four years a generation of college students will graduate with the basic proposition fixed in their minds that American culture is truly pluralistic. They may not be informed of the origins and functions of pluralism and its consequences for national life.

With so much emphasis on pluralism and ethnic diversity, there is a readiness to overlook its conflictual elements and to recast it as something more positive than it is. Cynthia Enloe states: "Of all the groups that men attach themselves to, ethnic groups seem the most encompassing and enduring. . . . Ethnicity . . . refers to a peculiar bond among persons that causes them to consider themselves a group distinguishable from others. . . . Ethnicity equips an individual with a sense of belonging: it positions him in society."[9]

Miss Enloe makes one believe that it is difficult to communicate with those outside one's ethnic group. For her, ethnicity is a limiting experience and a defining status. Data have not been adduced to show individuals happier in their ethnic group than out of it. For each fulfillment one finds in his ethnic group, a frustration can be found. But since it is not the purpose of some writers to discover the limitations of ethnicity, such evidence is often overlooked. Perhaps the following example will clarify what we mean.

In Eureka Springs, Arkansas in 1973, just one black person was a permanent resident of the town and the county. He had lived there more than fifty years. All blacks, including his family, had emigrated by the early 1950s. This lone black man decided to stay. In the early 1940s he went to Jefferson County, about three hundred miles away, to work in the war industry. He remained only a few days before returning to the mountains, from which he never again departed. He told the writer he could not adjust to Jefferson County, for there were just too many black people and he did not feel comfortable among them. His life was among his friends, all of whom were white. He said he had very little need or desire to be among people simply because they were black, that friendship is not limited to members of one's own race.

It seems that pluralism is no longer viewed as a hypothesis among some academics, but as a concrete reality to be communicated to the people. Pluralism and ethnicity appear to be mental constructs emerging from the preset attitudes of observers. Both are convenient, evident, easily concluded findings. But do they have solid empirical referents? They are used in private definitional ways. Their values as constants or variables cannot be determined, and so they lose their meanings as useful social predictors. Together they are like a genie in a bottle, to be summoned up whenever the owner/user wishes, to describe human relations within a politically acceptable framework.

But there is emerging a body of dissent to the pluralistic position. The observations of DeSantis and Benkins are pertinent:

Ethnicity, as expressed through the ethnic community and its associations, must of necessity conflict with the individual's participation in American society's major institutions. Not only does upward social mobility require more time in such institutions, but continued participation in the ethnic sub-society becomes even more obviously inconsistent, especially as it is attributed to a working—even lower-class status.[10]

They further observe: "It is clear that American society is supportive of cultural diversity if it is expressed in terms of art, food, and tradition. It is less acceptable if it involves obvious differences in religious expression or political activities."[11]

The census bureau and other population researchers are sometimes forced to place people in categories because so many are unable or unwilling to reveal their ethnic heritages. More and more are simply unable to say more than "I don't know."[12] Minority people may be quite unaware of their participation in the cultural pluralism argument and the consequences thereof. It is critical to the pluralist viewpoint to convince the minority, and therefore discriminated group, of the beauty and exclusiveness of its culture. The language, behavior, lifestyles, and values of the minority groups are changed from unacceptable to highly acceptable, by members of the ruling culture.

Some members of disesteemed groups may try to find value in their way of life so as not to suffer great relative deprivation in comparison with the major culture. Geneva Smitherman, in a recent article, argues that "Black English" is not poor grammar but is denied recognition because of the prejudice of the children's teachers.[13] Smitherman, unwittingly perhaps, does not understand that her claim for the validity of "Black English" is a pluralistic one and ultimately disadvantageous to black youth struggling to improve their competitive positions.

Ethnic peoples in America have not been very critical of their leadership. Consequently they have failed to scrutinize carefully the efforts and programs of those who profess to lead them. The hidden agenda of ethnic leaders such as Michael Novak, Nathan Glazer, and D. P. Moynihan has not been known, for it has been believed that if one were ethnic whatever was/is done is for the welfare of the ethnic group the person represents. This error of judgment has made it appear that leaders who are Polish, for example, are working on behalf of Poles and that Italian leaders are in support of the Italians, not other ethnic peoples. A Klansman often argues he is working for white people and not for himself.[14] Even grandiose schemes such as North Carolina's "Soul City" proved to be more a program for the aggrandizement of an individual than for black people at large. Really, are Jewish financial leaders primarily for the greater Jewry or for the lining of their own pockets?

It is probably closer to the truth to say that most Americans work for themselves rather than for their ethnic, racial, religious, or cultural groups. If they are leaders of these groups, their prosperity is often conspicuous, and suspicions are raised as to how they can prosper when the majority of their own people are locked in poverty. Legitimately, it is often claimed that leaders are simply using these groups for their own benefit.

Scholars like Toennies (gemeinschaft and gesellschaft) and Durkheim (mechanical and organic solidarity) have observed that society is moving from primary to secondary social relationships and from charismatic to bureaucratic social life. If these writers are correct, if relationships are becoming more impersonal, is it reasonable to expect a return to the face-to-face relationships of the old ethnic community and village? Will the community of a single ethnic culture contain the impersonal relationships of the larger city? If the ethnic community is impersonal and cold, what is the advantage for its participants? But it is suggested that there is security in the ethnic community when no such security exists.

When a choice is forced between the mobility of an individual or that of the ethnic group represented by that person, the group is sacrificed. Ethnicity simply has no strength unless it can be exploited by some individual or small group. Only small groups profit from ethnicity and any advantage bestowed by it. The majority of ethnics are slowly strangled by it. Indians, Anglos, blacks, and others individually chose more certain mobility for themselves rather than work for the more uncertain improvement of their particular groups.

The unwillingness of ethnic peoples, aside from blacks, to criticize their leaders or their programs prohibits the full understanding of the implications of the proposals. They evidently feel that their groups are closed corporations, large families whose dirty wash should not be hung out for all to see. The leaders are therefore able to take advantage of opportunities for their own gain while using the names and problems of the groups to their personal advantage. Black capitalism, for instance, was not a program for the general help of black people, but mainly for the benefit of a few of the most aggressive of black leaders. Likewise, other ethnic leaders somehow translate their interest in their group into personal gain while the persons they purport to represent make very modest gains or stagnate in the socioeconomic struggle for improvement. Again, it might be observed that poor whites inclined to accept the leadership of Klansmen remain poor while contributing to the enlargement of the Klan war chest. These funds usually disappear into the pockets of the leaders themselves. In many cases ethnicity and pluralism are simply social commodities for sale by rank hustlers and shysters. Ethnicity is a game well understood by people newly from Europe and other countries. In America, after trying to forget ethnicity, opportunists seek to turn back the clock to make America into the type of social nightmare Europe and other countries were, where race and ethnicity will once again be raised to significance.

13

THE DEPLURALIZATION OF BLACKS
AND OTHER GROUPS

By "depluralization" we mean the reduced emphasis of a minority group's priority of its social and cultural heritage. The group hereafter seeks absorption, rights, and responsibilities as an unidentifiable member of the host culture. No culture can expect to become vital if it fails to draw on the talent of the world. In ancient times great civilizations were never culturally isolated; they attracted people from everywhere. They recognized cultural differences but could not allow them to become paramount. Thus when too many Romans were found in Greece trying to establish an alternative culture, problems arose, for the Romans were changing the basic format of Greek culture. In modern America a similar condition exists. The vitality of America has been her ability to draw on the talent of the world and to change Old World allegiances in the process. Historically, groups entered America because they saw possibilities for better lives. The relative freedom they achieved enticed them to want to become a part of the American dream. The quicker they rid themselves of Old World behaviors, names, and trappings, the better.

By the middle of the 1970s entering groups had shifted their attitudes toward American culture. Just as many clamored to enter as ever, but they wanted to preserve their cultural uniqueness. Even old ethnic Americans began to turn back toward a worship of their Old World culture. All wanted the rights of American citizenship but did not want to be identified with American culture. This was not due wholly to their volition. Theoretical support for a separatist outlook began to assert itself. In this work we have tried to show how a philosophy of cultural and ethnic pluralism has attempted to displace the much older melting pot or assimilationist viewpoint. We have suggested that academics and intellectuals have promoted separatist strategies under the dogma of cultural pluralism.

While many ethnic groups are retreating into their own cultures, gearing up for political conflict, others are rushing forward to become encompassed in the American dream. Again, blacks were forced into a pluralistic stance by the facts of slavery and discrimination, but they fought through the courts and in the streets to reject separate status. They have defeated all attempts to classify them as non-Americans. They have gone, albeit in small numbers, to Africa, the Caribbean, South America, and even to Europe and the Orient, seeking empathy and unity with other people. They have sometimes been accepted, but in the final analysis they conclude that they and America are inseparable. It is this group which, in its effort to find its true identity in the American family, is probably doing most to depluralize America. It has not been an easy struggle. Their story merits reemphasis because other groups newer to this problem may profit from the black experience and be buoyed up by their dogged faith in America when pluralism threatens its very foundations.

Many American educational and political leaders have been quietly working to find legal ways of removing blacks from the American family. They are essentially in a process of undercutting their citizenship. Categories of differences are established and maintained between the Americans and other people. All significant social and economic data are broken down by black and white; I.Q. scores, political preference, religious and marriage choices, and a hundred others. The supposition is that there can be only one true American type, and that type must be white. Blacks, and all other nonwhites, if they are to be considered American at all, must be second class.

This arbitrary definition of Americanism has been contested at every point by groups unwilling to abide by such a supposition. The attack has come in the form of suits for civil rights, for there can be no citizenship responsibilities without the granting of civil rights. But segregationist strategy fails again and again in the courts, for it is impossible to prove that long-time dwellers in the country are not citizens. Yet de facto categorization by race continues because there is still hope by some that enough differences will be found between the groups to disqualify blacks from citizenship and opportunity. Few politicians are willing to admit the unqualified equality of all citizens.

In most of the rest of the world racial categories have been practically abolished. Few studies are conducted which utilize race as a variable. This is not to ignore, of course, that race is still important in many countries. But almost all official policy is aimed at decreasing its emphasis.

America remains the principal country where studies utilize race as a major social category. Most countries have such a few social scientists or outlets for their research that opportunities to bring forward a focus on racial categories are small. Within the past few years, however, scholars influenced by American race relations have nearly succeeded in raising race to political significance in other countries by using ethnicity as a substitute for race. Although they are not the only ones, Nathan Glazer and Daniel P. Moynihan have risen to the top of the heap arguing the vitality of ethnicity in such works as *Ethnicity: Theory and Experience* (1974). What was formerly considered racial conflict is simply redefined as ethnic conflict.

Where categories exist, there must be facilities and activities to correspond to them. If the categories are fictitious, the facilities created will be fictitious. Racial categories are always arbitrary and political, and they bear little relationship to social reality. They are forced, illegal categories, unreal from any but political and power viewpoints. Thus, where white and black categories exist, they have much to do with the adjustment of these groups to the positions envisioned for them by those instrumental in the establishment or preservation of the categories.

A people cannot become depluralized unless it changes its attitudes toward itself as it relates to its host country. The Old Immigrants from western Europe found it a practical necessity to deemphasize cultural connections to their mother countries. Had they preferred to remain in their own limited cultural environments, at a time when the Anglos had a head start on them, they probably would never have become competitive and eventually might have become the servants of the peoples of English background. They could not remain nationalities and Americans at the same time. The transition was probably difficult for the older members but easier for their children. If the country had been socially, economically, or culturally partitioned, as was the case in many countries of Europe, the task would have been relatively easy. Newcomers would simply have taken up living in the areas where their fellow ethnics resided. But America was hostile toward the establishment of separate cultures. There had always been fear and suspicion of other cultures, especially when their workings were unknown. Value judgments were made against the separate groups. The majority culture could ask, "What is so wrong with our way of doing things? If it is good enough for everyone else, what makes you or your group so special?" New and immigrant cultures were hard pressed to offer plausible answers, and it soon became obvious that "they think they are superior to us."

Once this conclusion is reached, the stage is set for conflict between the groups. In America groups may fail to integrate for practically any reason except the implication that someone or some group is fundamentally "better than another." Perhaps the one value ground into practically every American is the notion that "one person is as good as another." Any hint of deviation from that idea sets off reactions of the gravest sorts. Unlike other countries, America has no meaningful division of the population into a "we"-"they" dichotomy. The culture is crosscut and it is practically impossible to block up people according to certain beliefs and ideologies. An unknown bard put the issue clearly:

How do Americans see things?
It is very hard to say,
For on many they are we,
And on just as many we are they.

Differences among Americans are more conceptual: they are of degree rather than of kind. Democrats are not really different from Republicans. Jews and Christians are not really different, nor are blacks and whites. Differences and preferences are minimized when anything of national consequence is at stake, which attests to the essential "oneness" of American values. If there were a true plurality of cultures, it would require strong police action to assure united effort in times of national crisis. Very few subversives were discovered during World War 2, even though millions of Germans and Italians were found in the general population. The erroneous internment of the Japanese of the West Coast illustrated that they were more American than even the sociologists thought. Some younger militant Japanese-Americans of the latter generations, moved by the experience of their parents, continue to demand retribution from the U.S. government. But, by and large, the American people have all but forgotten the incident and assigned the error to understandable mistakes made under the hysteria of war. As before the war, the Japanese-Americans have shown by their industry and citizenship that they do not need the artificial props of ethnic identity to help them become successful in society. There has been no major test comparable to the Japanese example of the extent to which newer groups have depluralized to see themselves as Americans rather than as representatives of some other nationalities. Almost everyone, scholars included, failed to estimate the effect of America in producing one people from a conglomeration of nationalities. Even the Mexican War failed to generate permanent hostility against the Americans among the rank and file Mexican people. If anything, the war resulted in the sharing of cultures to a greater extent, so that today modern Mexico City is very much like any great American city and Mexicans of the mainstream are very much like Americans of the middle class.

Newer immigrants have not had to make the same types of choices regarding their pluralized status as their parents. Entering the economic system at a time when it was more developed and predictable than before, immigrants have not had to test their commitment to American values. Because of the openness of the culture, newcomers believe they may easily establish replicas of their home cultures in America with little more than an economic tie. No crisis has forced a decision. The idea is therefore perpetuated that the newer groups are under no compulsion to depluralize, that America is neutral about its inundation with peoples of other cultures when there is little commitment by them to greater American values.

Depluralization is seen as a strategy for blacks who are trying to escape discrimination, but not for other groups which wish to retain their cultures even though to do so means less than full access to all America has to offer. But an emphasis on the retention of Old World culture obscures the actual cost of the separatist position to the pluralists.

Old World ethnics now accept their lots meekly; few fight to open up the society for all. Instead they form to make gains for their own groups, for their vision does not extend to the freedom of all of whatever color or station in life. If the Italians can control the ash dump of Chicago, the Poles the boneyards, and the Greeks the hot dog vending market, they will not contest the running of the large businesses and government by the "true Americans." All will retire nightly to their separate ghettos, hating the Jews for their book learning and despising the blacks for not being happy with their monopoly of domestic work and the muscle trades. Most of all they will hate themselves for not being Anglo.[1]

There is no better example of the depluralization process than that of black Americans who early on had to address the question of whether they would be separate or integrated Americans. There were few modern models for them to follow, for nowhere else had such a large number of people of one race and of substantially different culture been forced to accept the culture of an oppressor group. The problem remained until the issue was at least partially solved by the Civil War.

The status of blacks complicated that of all immigrants, for their own position could not become clarified until some acceptable political and social disposition was made of the black case. It took a long time, from Reconstruction through 1954, to gain a clear idea of the direction of the movement of black people within the context of the American family. The period of official segregation, dating from the *Plessy* decision of 1896, and the subsequent development of some relatively prosperous black institutions, enabled the false belief to arise that black and while cultures could function acceptably if separated. The long-time accommodationism of Booker T. Washington, the nationalism of Marcus Garvey, and the recalcitrance of the U.S. Supreme Court in judging citizenship fairly, led to a feeling that pluralism or separatism was the natural state of black and white Americans. But this idea was sharply attacked by those with a vision of one America.

There have remained many reminders of the strength of ethnicity and race even though they no longer have force as legal realities. It is not certain that social scientists have not added to the longevity of pluralism by believing so strongly in it when it is known that the concept is a learned one. As race and ethnicity were created (they do not exist in nature), so may they be destroyed. If there were needs or uses for them in the past, these needs are no longer present, especially in America. To continue with them, even on a scholarly basis, reflects deep pluralistic socialization which might easily confuse one's understanding of social reality.

The legal changes of the past score of years have created a new number of the American family, though he has been a very old contender. In the 1920s and 1930s Alain Locke could speak of the "New Negro." By that he meant that the black American had taken a new stand toward his own heritage. In the depths of despair and rejection by the larger society, he began to reinterpret his experiences and force them to become part of the American heritage. The Harlem Renaissance was the popular expression of this reinterpretation. Attitudes changed, and a new pride in black heritage erupted. Black songs, art, and literature reflected that he no longer saw himself as merely a deprived person without rights or humanity within a white-dominated society. But if whites did not want him as a full partner, then he would turn his frustration inward, redirect it, and build a society of his own, on the foundations of his own culture. It would be so expressive, natural, and desirable that those who rejected blacks would themselves feel rejected if they were completely alienated from this new culture. Thus the thing for the most liberal whites to do was to go to Harlem on weekends to enjoy jazz and the tasty folk foods, to look in amazement at the impact of a rejected rural people upon a mighty ethnocentric culture. And soon white culture took over aspects of black culture, incorporating it into its own fabric, giving up aspects of its own culture in return.

World War 2 redirected the Harlem Renaissance. The demands of the economy for labor, fighting men, and support forces compelled America to draw upon the reservoir of blacks to help execute the war. In so doing, America opened the way for greater black demands for full citizenship during and after the war. Gains made toward full citizenship, however few persons were involved, inevitably chipped away at the foundation of segregation on which the entire structure rested, weakening it drastically. More persons were asking for rights as citizens, not just as blacks.

In the 1950s, for the first time in the history of the country, there was a court, the Warren Court, which began to interpret the Constitution without reference to the color of the litigants. The landmark decisions of *Brown* v. *Board of Education of Topeka, Miranda, Shelly* v. *Kraemer, Loving* v. *Virginia, Gomillion* v. *Lightfoot,* and others, were decisions which changed the face of race relations, not only in the United States but nearly everywhere in the Western world.

Everywhere the barriers against the free exercise of citizenship were falling, and race became one of the weakest grounds for the denial of citizenship rights. For a time the courts were most active in asserting that race meant little and that no citizen would be penalized because of race or ethnicity. The crowning expression of court disapproval of race was seen in 1972 in *Furman* v. *Georgia,* when the court held that as it was presently applied, capital punishment constituted cruel and unusual punishment and was therefore unconstitutional. It was known that the majority of prisoners on death row were black and that the death penalty was used disproportionately against blacks everywhere in the country, but especially throughout the South.

As barriers continued to fall on every front, the category of black, or Negro, was stripped of any meaning either may have had. A person could pick his own race, for it had no legal meaning. No penalty could be assessed because of race; however, consideration could be given to a person who was making every effort to overcome the handicaps of race. In that sense, the substantial financial help, learning programs, and so on, which were extended to blacks, were for the purpose of helping them overcome the disability of race, not to make the separatist concept meaningful. Of course, some thought the latter was the purpose, and the cry was raised that blacks were being given preference over whites, which itself was in violation of the Constitution. White backlashes developed, especially against those institutions which played the largest role in bringing persons into citizenship: the schools. Kindergarten and Head Start programs proliferated. They were preceded by better prenatal care which would try to help assure that black youngsters would not start off their lives with the physical and psychological handicaps of their predecessors.

The logic behind these moves, while viewed as placatory by some, since many followed the riots of the 1960s, was quite simple. Noncitizenship was unproductive and costly. The quicker blacks could be brought into the American family on a productive basis so that special help was not required, the better off all would be. There would be fewer jagged nerves and social problems.

The legal changes have certainly brought about behavior changes in various ethnic categories. More people are working together, living in the same communities, and socializing with greater frequency and less tension than was dreamed possible a generation ago. The younger and better educated whites and blacks are able to relate to each other in more genuine ways.

Pessimists and primordialists, however, will claim that this close inter-action does not mean a change of psychology on the part of either the blacks or the whites; that at bottom they remain antagonistic, nervously awaiting the time when old animosities will burst to the fore.[2] There remain indeed many reminders of the strength of ethnicity and race, even though the latter no longer have force as legal realities. It is difficult to erase a concept, to generate a new system of thought, when there are so many reminders of it, even informal ones.

While blacks are becoming depluralized, other groups are asking for recognition of their cultures on the basis of their uniqueness and separate-ness. In some cities there are identifiable new ghettos peopled largely by ethnic groups such as the Hispanic Armourdale district of greater Kansas City. The Cubans have gained enough political strength in Miami to boast of their ability to provide services which stretch from the cradle to the grave. Some cities of the Southwest have taken on a similar character with respect to Mexicans and Chicanos. Few other recent immi-grants have been able to stake out territory and control it by the sheer weight of numbers and a self-contained economy. But ethnic strongholds of older European immigrants exist in some of the larger eastern cities and threaten to become separatist with the encouragement by their current ethnic leaders.

The control of certain cities, or part of them, by Latin peoples coin-cides with the takeover of political control of other large cities by blacks. While it makes these formerly, and to a large extent presently, excluded people feel much better to say they have leaders of their own ethnicity in charge, very little has changed for their own rank and file. Things may have grown worse. Under the former arrangement, when whites were in control, at least one could yell discrimination when services were not delivered. Under ethnic leadership, when services are not delivered there can be little excuse, because "your leaders are your own people."

Black people have experienced corruption and failure of leadership within the ghetto and understand that a community cannot be viable when it is cut off from the strength of the larger society. Leaders like Coleman Young of Detroit, Gibson of Newark, and Hatcher of Gary have learned this lesson. A change in the complexion of leadership does not usher in greater prosperity or more efficient services for all the people. Some individuals will prosper, but the economies of the cities will decline if they are run for the benefit of any particular group or class. Corruption accompanies efforts to cater principally to the whims of specific groups, as we have seen in many of the African countries.

Ethnic leadership is no magnetic pull to ethnic people. Japanese did not flock to San Francisco State University when S. I. Hayakawa was appointed president. Blacks of great qualifications are not rushing to Detroit or Gary or East St. Louis where the economies are slowing down. People of all qualifications (and colors) do seem to be headed for New Orleans and Los Angeles where black mayors preside, but only because there are more jobs. All recognize it is not the color of the face of the city leader but the opportunity to prosper which provides the pull. Blacks would be the first to dismiss their mayors if they ever attempted to administer their cities by exclusive appeal to the racial and ethnic urges of their constituents.

The single-ethnicity town or city seldom reaches the heights of vitality. Too many of its resources must be used to placate those assisting the leaders to remain in power. According to our research there is not a prosperous town in America which is peopled by a single ethnic group, not even a town with a population 100 percent Anglo. A mix of people seems to be required, and in the process they move toward adoption of a more uniform standard of culture.

The late nineteenth and first half of the twentieth centuries were devoted to discovering ways of Americanizing black people after they escaped from the shackles of slavery. This task was undertaken with considerable ambivalence, for some 250 years of bondage had led some to think of blacks as unfit for full citizenship. But the die was cast; the Civil War was fought to clarify the status of blacks. Even then there were those who failed to understand the full citizenship of the former slaves. For some one hundred years after the war, blacks periodically moved closer to full citizenship; then, just as precipitously, it was snatched away. This was one feature of life which was played with for decades by all political leaders as a ball of string is toyed with by a kitten. It seemed to be a very hard lesson to learn that once citizenship was promised, granted, or provided for in the law, it could not be denied.

The slave experience and its one hundred year aftermath had a great impact on the psychology of all Americans, and the rest of the world. It was something none could easily overcome, and it tended to literally control the thoughts of Martin Luther King's "sons of slaves and sons of slave masters." No aspect of America could be discussed, planned, or envisioned without an inevitable allusion to the position of our darker brothers. And for a long time even black scholars such as E. F. Frazier, W. E. B. DuBois, and J. H. Franklin, to name just a few, took as their starting points of analyses the former slave status of blacks. For the nonacademic black, lurking behind every freedom was the suspicion that it was not real, that "white folks are just putting us on." Fear had created a person hesitant about his own freedom, for it placed him in a new and unpredictable relationship to all of those who formerly outranked him. Three hundred years of subjugation was mind-warping for both the blacks and their former masters. It was easier to think in terms of the old categories. Just as most blacks see limitations for themselves, many whites likewise still see blacks with severe limitations and themselves with extensive privileges.

The Americanization of blacks was the central item on the social agenda long before the issue of immigrant assimilation came to the fore. There was something wrong with newcomers becoming assimilated, or even gaining recognition, ahead of persons who were already in the country. That noncitizens could be pushed ahead of citizens of a generation's standing was explicable only by reference to very confused ideas and politics of the time. This could be rationalized only if all parties concerned decided to see black people as odd men out instead of as ordinary American citizens deserving all rights and responsibilities. As individuals there might be outstanding black people who would demand and achieve equal rights, but rethinking would be required to bring the entire black category to this status.

There is still substantial, if subtle, discrimination against blacks by white communities, associations, businesses, and professions—especially in the field of real estate. With blacks insisting on their own cultural forms, even as a reaction to discrimination, it is easy to grant them separation, thereby encouraging further discrimination. Earlier segregation was forced; now it is sometimes chosen by the discriminated group. They may be manipulated by those with a deep interest in their separation from the rest of American society. If it is asserted that there is a viable black culture, a demand must be made to preserve it. If there is no black culture, one must admit that it was destroyed during slavery and that the black element was not strong enough to withstand more than three centuries of mistreatment. But this is tantamount to saying that blacks were defeated by whites during slavery. Such a position cannot be maintained in the face of the "strength of black culture" thesis. The position becomes self-contradictory.

Blacks and whites, for all the actual and imputed hostility which exists between them in the U.S., are perhaps the most likely allies as we move into the area of ethnicity over and above that required for the normal maintenance of social identity. No two groups know as much about each other as American blacks and whites. Quite often they are as close together as blood will allow. Not far back in antiquity their roots are entangled to the extent they are indistinguishable. Even today interracial courtship and marriage rates are higher by far between whites and native blacks than between whites and any of the darker immigrants. This certainly proves that the groups are not far apart ideologically, culturally, or physically.

As improbable as it may seem, if there is a natural coalition anywhere in America, it is that of blacks and whites. Heavy propaganda has prevented this from becoming widely understood. Blacks and whites have worked together to build this country, even when unequally yoked. They fought together to free it from England, to defend it from secessionism in the Civil War. They spilt blood together at San Juan Hill and shared bloody bandages during the two holocausts of world wars where they fought and died to disprove the myth of one race's superiority over another. All subsequent skirmishes with foreign powers have found blacks and whites disproportionately giving their lives, each conceptualizing the struggles in different terms, but each realizing that whatever the outcome, America and they (blacks and whites) were inseparable. They are and cannot be other than one.

Immigrants cannot feel toward either native blacks or whites as these groups feel about each other. The outward signs may be hatred, but the spiritual feeling is love. That's just the way it is; history has made it so. Thus it is impossible for foreigners to encroach upon American whites without activating the deep sense of fairness and forgiveness in the hearts of blacks. For somewhere in that white skin is a part of someone dark, a little bit of that slave who gained his freedom through an accidental combination of genes. And every white person knows that every black person is no more nor less than that darker, hidden side of himself, a side he can no more ignore than his own brother, a side that forever threatens to break out, unless prohibited by the force of law or custom, to fully embrace all that the black brother embraces, because love and blood and a fundamental belief in equality, right, and fair play, tie them together.

CONCLUDING REMARKS

In this book I have looked at the issue of cultural pluralism from a variety of perspectives and considered several topics which have a bearing on the issue. I believe several concluding remarks are justified. The melting pot has come under attack lately, not because it is no longer the predominant and working social philosophy of America, but because of attempts to placate groups according to assessments of their actual or potential political influence. Groups have discovered ways of translating their numerical strength into political gain under the cover of cultural pluralism. All groups are becoming more selfish and less interested in the common good. But encouragement for the pluralistic philosophy is coming at a time when it is critical that America reassess its own status as a country with great social meaning for the rest of the world. Events of the past few years indicate that there is a growing dislike of America by foreign governments. One might conjecture that some new nationality groups in the U.S. may have greater loyalty to their old lands than to their new home. This is a significant change in the attitudes of immigrants toward their newly adopted country. They are willing to come to America for the economic gains they may make but they are very much like migrant agricultural workers who have no commitment to the protection of the fields or crops they work, or to the employers who hire them. Their relationship is economic—for them, emotional investment in the situation is not necessary. Likewise, newer immigrant peoples, without a basic stake in the freedom and prosperity of America cannot feel it is their country. It is not an issue for them that all citizens must be protected with the same full rights they take for granted. Americans of old standing have long understood that there cannot be an America divided artificially by practice, culture, or philosophy. They find it unsettling to distribute men into higher and lower estates. While persons from other countries may not yet be familiar with the theory of equality, those of generations' standing in America understand it fully. Protection of freedom may be advocated most strongly by those most thoroughly internalizing it. Their faith in unity is being undercut by scholars and politicians espousing pluralism. But such divisions may be considered normal in countries characterized by many artificially created social groups.

A struggle is now in progress to redefine the social meaning of America. This is not apparent to everyone but should be to those who closely study and observe the country. This struggle has resulted in the division of America into two hostile camps: assimilationist and pluralist. Assimilationists are derided by pluralists as integrationists, mongrelists, communists, etc., while assimilationists call pluralists segregationists, Klansmen, and doubtless many other names.

Fundamentally, assimilationists are simply believers in the idea that the darker and newer peoples of America should become full and equal partners in the drama of national history. They feel that this is the only philosophy that will ensure the preservation of America as a distinctly prosperous and fair society; they believe their concept comes closest to producing equity in regard to things which all men hold dear; and they reject the notion that there can be peace without harmony and without general agreement on basic values. The "oneness" of mankind is the bedrock assimilationist teaching.

At the other extreme are the pluralists. The cornerstone of their program is their belief that mankind comes in many packages, separated in such a way that their contents can never and should never mix. For them men are grouped into broad categories by race, ethnicity, religion, or status. Separation is further produced in each of these categories and, under fragmentation, groups and individuals strive to protect even the smallest differences between themselves and others. Preservation of separation at all costs is the clarion call of the pluralist.

Many people, of course, have not made up their minds which group to follow, both sides are struggling to gain position and converts. But the stakes are higher for the country at large than for private individuals. Individuals may use their uniqueness to cancel out the consequences of prejudices. Assimilationists may be forced, out of necessity, to work with pluralists who advocate apartheid. Pluralists, in powerless positions, may be compelled to survive in the midst of assimilationists. It is thus quite difficult to know what an individual's stand is. Yet it is clear that the consequences for the country will be different if it formally adopts either an assimilationist or pluralist program.

America has had some experience in the practical application of both these philosophies. When half of the country, the South, tried to apply rank pluralism (slavery and segregation), it failed for more than three hundred years to achieve general prosperity and harmony. The ghettoization of white ethnics and their discrimination in the North slowed down the nation's development.

Assimilation was the original idea dominating the country, and it was defended on pragmatic and humanitarian grounds. White Protestants from northern Europe assimilated more rapidly than the darker Catholics of eastern and southern Europe. The other dark peoples from other parts of the world, and some North American indigenes, would have to wait much longer to assimilate until their culture more closely lived up to white standards. When efforts were made to allocate status by race or caste, the method failed. American culture, regardless of practice, dictated the recognition of talent wherever and in whatever group it occurred. Categorical denial of status and opportunity to individuals of the wrong race or caste could be maintained only by artificial means. Talent was found in roughly the same proportions in each group, and only a different opportunity structure propped up by the separatist teachings of pluralism would keep talent from being recognized.

Pluralism means that the economy cannot function at maximum productivity. It creates a split-labor market,[1] and, we might add, a split-consumer market. Production and consumption are related; earning power and buying power are related. A split-labor market is one in which the labor of one group is not competitive with another. The group receiving the lower wages cannot purchase the items produced by those given preference in the wage-labor structure. The privileged group must hold down its production to conform to the demands of a limited group of consumers, which has a depressing effect on the general economy.

Cultural pluralism cannot be divorced from ethnicity. It is around ethnicity that much conflict has swirled. European immigrants to the New World were immediately in conflict with Indians, who represented a different culture. Successive waves of immigrants settled apart, carving out their religious, linguistic, and ethnic ghettos in the wilderness. Differences between Old World groups were great, and few were tied together simply by the accident of common nationality or language. A low German was no more accepted by a high German than an Irishman was by an Englishman.

Pluralists vigorously deny that out of this hodgepodge of great cultural differences emerged one people. Their logic depicts America as a land of warring and hostile tribes of unsolvable cultural differences. Such a position is maintained despite the fact that, historically, nearly all government programs have, until recently, been aimed at reducing societal conflict by minimizing the material and even ideological differences between groups, and not without success.

Cultural pluralism and ethnicity have become intellectually confused. I have tried to separate them conceptually, but, practically, the task has not been accomplished. Perhaps it is not possible to do so. Neither cultural nor ethnic groups holding themselves apart have been treated as equal in America because the two are so closely related. Each is a separate people. The cultural and ethnic groups are stratified, and in that process they become classes, castes, and finally races. They add to the emerging confusion which the country seeks to avoid.

Ethnic manipulators, scholars, politicians, and thought-brokers have planted the virus and created a fever of ethnicity in the U.S.[2] In their praise of this malady they have failed to point out the serious limitations of blind adherence to ethnic culture. The boundaries of ethnic culture are reached very quickly, while there are practically no limits on those of the mainstream. A Jewish writer can write only about the Jewish condition, which is a subset of the human condition—important, but small in comparison to the total human experience. Jesse Owens would not want to be honored as a great *black* runner, for he fits into the context of a great Olympian without any tag of ethnicity. Zubin Mehta would be insulted to be limited to recognition as an *Indian* musical genius. Accomplished and secure individuals do not need the security blanket of ethnicity. By contrast, threatened persons seek to convert the weaknesses of the ethnic group in order to gain primary group strengths which it never had and perhaps never can, by itself, produce. It is therefore difficult to expect very intelligent, learned, and secure individuals to be loyal to an ethnic group. Ethnicity makes many demands, conceals weaknesses, and offers few genuine rewards for obedience to it.

Ethnic groups in America usually remain pluralistic out of fear. They are trying to preserve their precarious positions in what is, or is perceived as, a hostile social environment. None has successfully resisted the pull of the larger modern culture, when perceived as desirable and fair. And those who remain ethnic are probably as unhappy and unfulfilled as those renegades who made a break from it.

America is not a good place for cultural pluralism and ethnicity to flourish. It defeats all efforts of individuals or groups to remain separate. Cultural pluralism seems to have very little future in America in the long run.

NOTES

INTRODUCTION

1. See *Congressional Record,* 69th Cong., 2nd Sess., January 18, 1927, p. 1904.
2. A. R. Jensen's "How Much Can We Boost I.Q. and Scholastic Achievement?" *Harvard Educational Review* 39 (1969): 1–123 revived the issue, substantially, as a political one. There are scholars who held to genetic explanations of social differences years before Jensen. Among these were Audrey M. Shuey, *The Testing of Negro Intelligence* (Lynchburg, Va.: J. B. Bell Co., 1958), Carlton Putnam, *Race and Reason* (Washington: Public Affairs Press, 1961), and Wesley C. George, *The Biology of the Race Problem* (Commission of the Governor of Alabama, 1962).
3. Milton Gordon, *Assimilation in American Life* (New York: Oxford University Press, 1964), gives an excellent summary of the various theoretical and practical approaches to the issue of new people in America.
4. William J. Wilson, *The Declining Significance of Race: Blacks and Changing American Institutions* (Chicago: University of Chicago Press, 1978), is probably the leading proponent of the idea that lower class status is holding black people down more than objective discrimination. Charles V. Willie has sharply criticized Wilson's position in "The Inclining Significance of Race," *Society,* (July–August, 1978).

1: ATTACKS ON THE MELTING POT

1. Milton Gordon, *Assimilation in American Life* (New York: Oxford University Press, 1964), p. 90.
2. Ibid., pp. 92–93.
3. Ibid., p. 96.
4. Ibid., p. 97.
5. See William Petersen, *Japanese Americans* (New York: Random House, 1971), pp. 39–40; also Stanford M. Lyman, *Chinese Americans* (New York: Random House, 1974).
6. Edward Shils, translator, ed. *Max Weber on Universities: The Power of the State and the Dignity of the Academic Calling in Imperial Germany* (Chicago: University of Chicago Press, 1974), p. 2.

7. See "Loss of Magnetism of White Culture," in Gordon D. Morgan, *The Ghetto College Student: A Descriptive Essay on College Youth from the Inner City* (Iowa City, Iowa: The American College Testing Program, 1970), pp. 11–14.

8. Brewton Berry, *Race and Ethnic Relations* (Boston: Houghton Mifflin, 1951), p. 249.

9. George E. Simpson and J. M. Yinger, *Racial and Cultural Minorities: An Analysis of Prejudice and Discrimination*, 3rd ed. (New York: Harper & Row, 1965), p. 6.

10. Nathan Glazer and Daniel Patrick Moynihan, *Beyond the Melting Pot: The Negroes, Puerto Ricans, Jews, Italians, and Irish of New York City* (Cambridge, Mass.: The M.I.T. Press, 1963), pp. 14–15.

11. Ibid., p. 17.

12. Ibid., p. 18.

13. Ibid., p. 12.

14. Berry, p. 251.

15. Melvin Steinfield, *Cracks in the Melting Pot* 2nd ed. (New York: Glencoe Press, 1973), pp. 262–65.

16. Harold Fruchtbaum, review, *Change* (March–April, 1971), p. 69.

17. Robert S. Lynd and Helen M. Lynd, *Middletown* (New York: Harcourt, Brace, 1929); James West, *Plainville, U.S.A.* (New York: Columbia University Press, 1945). Of the many works detailing American religious intolerance see Earl Raab, *Religious Conflict in America* (Garden City, N.Y.: Anchor Books, Doubleday and Company, 1964).

18. Isaac Berkson, *Theories of Americanization: A Critical Study* (New York: Teachers College, Columbia University, 1920).

19. Thomas Pettigrew, "Racially Separate or Together," in Edgar G. Epps, ed., *Cultural Pluralism* (Berkeley, Calif.: McCutchan, 1974), p. 24.

20. On the pathologies of the ghetto, see William Moore, Jr., *The Vertical Ghetto* (New York: Random House, 1969), and K. B. Clark, *Dark Ghetto* (New York: Harper & Row, 1965).

21. Andrew T. Kopan, "The Melting Pot: Myth or Reality?" in Epps, p. 53.

22. About 20 percent of American whites are estimated to be descendants of persons of African origin. Robert Stuckert, "African Ancestry of the White American Population" *Ohio Journal of Science* 58, no. 3 (May 1958): 155ff.

23. William J. Wilson, *The Declining Significance of Race: Blacks and Changing American Institutions* (Chicago: University of Chicago Press, 1978).

24. Alfredo Castaneda, "Persisting Ideological Issues of Assimilation in America," in Epps, p. 56.

25. Reed Ueda, "The Americanization and Education of Japanese-Americans," in Epps, pp. 77–90.

26. Barbara A. Sizemore, "Making the Schools a Vehicle for Cultural Pluralism," in Epps, p. 100.

27. Judson Hixon, "Community Control: The Values behind a Call for Change," in Epps, p. 119.

28. Edward J. Barnes, "The Utilization of Behavioral and Scoial Sciences in Minority Group Education," in Epps, p. 139.

29. Epps, p. 179.

30. Melvin M. Tumin and Walter Plotch, eds., *Pluralism in a Democratic Society* (New York: Praeger, 1977).

31. James P. Comer, "The Social Power of the Negro," *Scientific American* (April 1967): 21–27.

2: THEORIES AND PLURALISM

1.   Harold M. Hodges, Jr., *Social Stratification: Class in America* (Cambridge, Mass.: Schenkman, 1964), pp. 8–10.
2.   Lewis Killian and Charles Grigg, "Racial Crisis in America: Leadership in Conflict," in E. S. Greenberg, N. Milner, and D. J. Olson, *Black Politics* (New York: Holt, Rinehart & Winston, 1971), p. 293.
3.   Gunnar Myrdal, *An American Dilemma* (New York: Harper & Row, 1944).
4.   Joseph Himes, "The Functions of Racial Conflict," *Social Forces* 45, no. 1 (September 1966): 1–10, and his *Racial Conflict in American Society* (Columbus, Ohio: Charles E. Merrill Publishing Co., 1973).
5.   Vine Deloria, Jr., "The White Man's Problem," in *Viewpoints: Red and Yellow, Black and Brown* (Minneapolis, Minn.: Winston Press, 1972), p. 175.
6.   Ibid., p. 178.
7.   See David R. Hunter, *The Slums* (New York: Free Press, 1968), and Charles Abrams, *The City is the Frontier* (New York: Harper & Row, Colophon Books, 1967).

3: THE RISE OF THE ETHNIC MANIPULATORS

1.   Critics of the idea that blacks could enter very late in the game and become monopoly capitalists are E. F. Frazier, *The Black Bourgeoisie* (New York: Free Press, 1957) and Andrew Brimmer "Black Capitalism," *South Today* 1 (March 1970).
2.   John W. Smith and Bette W. Smith, "Desegregation in the South and the Demise of the Black Educator," *Journal of Social and Behavioral Sciences* 20, no. 1 (winter 1974): 33–40.
3.   Michael Novak, "The Seventies: Decade of the Ethnics," in R. J. Meister, ed., *Race and Ethnicity in Modern America* (Lexington, Mass.: D. C. Heath & Co., 1974), p. 144.
4.   Ibid., pp. 137–47.
5.   Charles Keil, "Urban Blues," in Meister, p. 108.
6.   Whites reportedly go through the stages of contentment, indignation, awkwardness, and dismay in interracial work. See C. J. Levy, *Voluntary Servitude* (New York: Appleton-Century-Crofts, 1968).
7.   A. D. Lavender and J. M. Forsyth, "The Sociological Study of Minority Groups as Reflected by Leading Sociological Journals: Who Gets Studied and Who Gets Neglected?" in *Ethnicity* 3, no. 4 (December 1976): 388–98, and in F. J. Davis, *Understanding Minority-Dominant Relations: Sociological Contributions* (Arlington Heights, Ill.: AHM Publishing Corporation, 1979), p. 6.
8.   Davis, p. 13, quoting from *Ethnicity* 1 (1974): 207.
9.   O. C. Cox, *Caste, Class and Race: A Study in Social Dynamics* (Garden City, N.Y.: Doubleday, 1948). See also his "Jewish Self-Interest in Black Pluralism," *Sociological Quarterly* 15, no. 2 (spring 1974): 183–98, and "The Question of Pluralism," *Race* 12, no. 4 (1971): 385–400.
10.   A bibliography of the work of Cox was done by Professor Hubert Ross of Atlanta University. It is reprinted in Gordon D. Morgan, "In Memoriam: Oliver C. Cox, 1901–1974," *Monthly Review* 28, no. 1 (1976): 34–40.
11.   Indirect rule is a system in which a few elitists utilize indigenous institutions and hierarchies to control the people while reaching individual and colonial

goals in the process. It was practiced widely in Africa and made popular by Frederick Lugard in northern Nigeria. For an appreciation of the use of the practice, see Donald L. Weidner, *A History of Africa: South of the Sahara* (New York: Vintage Books, 1962), pp. 252-57.

4: THE FALLACY OF CULTURAL PLURALISM

1. Frank Niger, "The New African Myths," *Transition* (East Africa) (September–October, 1964): 14-17. Roughly, these slogans mean togetherness, though they are applied in different parts of Africa. Jomo Kenyatta, late president of Kenya, used "harambee" to admonish Kenyans to pull together as a united group. In West Africa Leopold Senghor, president of Senegal, made famous the concept "Negritude," meaning the spiritual unity of black people. President Julius Nyerere of Tanzania popularized the term "ugamaa," meaning familyhood.

5: DISABILITIES AND THE MELTING POT

1. Gordon has noted a number of subprocesses of assimilation: behavioral and structural. In general, the former refers to immigrant acceptance of ideas, values, and cultural patterns of the host society, while the latter refers to entrance of the immigrants into the cliques, organizational life, and other structures of the host culture. Milton Gordon, *Assimilation and American Life* (New York: Oxford University Press, 1964).
2. In 1974 the median black family income was $7,808 compared to $13,356 for whites. The poverty line was established at an income of $5,038 per year for a nonfarm family of four (Leonard Broom and Philip Selznick, *Sociology,* 6th ed. [New York: Harper & Row, 1977], pp. 163 and 475). Because such a large proportion of blacks are below or only slightly above the poverty category, they are included in the lower class.
3. Michael Novak notes that ethnic Americans had yearly family incomes of between $5,000 and $10,000 in 1970. The chief wage-earner in the family hits a permanent income plateau by his early 30s, and from year to year life becomes a treadmill of grubbing and frustration. Cited in Robert Alter, "A Fever of Ethnicity," in David R. Colburn and George E. Pozzetta, eds., *America and the New Ethnicity* (Port Washington, N.Y.: Kennikat Press, 1979), p. 188. The immigrant experience is far from a romantic one. See W. I. Thomas and Florian Znaniecki, *The Polish Peasant in Europe and America* (New York: Dover Publications, 1958), and Oscar Handlin, *Immigration as a Factor in American History* (Englewood Cliffs, N.J.: Prentice-Hall, 1959).
4. Harold R. Isaacs, *Idols of the Tribe: Group Identity and Political Change* (New York: Harper & Row, 1977).
5. Consciousness of kind, according to Giddings, is a state of consciousness in which any being recognizes another conscious being as of like kind. . . . Consciousness of kind is a pleasurable state of mind which includes organic (subconscious) sympathy, the perception of resemblance, reflective sympathy, and the desire for recognition. See in N. S. Timasheff, *Sociological Theory: Its Nature and Growth,* 3rd ed. (New York: Random House, 1967), pp. 83-84.
6. Warner's influence on stratification studies has been great. For a concise review of his work and its theoretical significance, see Joel B. Montague, Jr., *Class and Nationality: English and American Studies* (New Haven, Conn.: College and University Press, 1963), pp. 38-43. One of the most lucid critiques of the caste school is found in O. C. Cox, *Caste, Class and Race* (Garden City, N.Y.: Doubleday, 1948).

7.   This theme is the organizing one in Irving Goffman, *Stigma: Notes on the Management of a Spoiled Identity* (Englewood Cliffs, N.J.: Prentice-Hall, 1963).

7: ETHNIC COMMUNITIES

1.   Although immigrants came to America seeking better lives, few escaped the bitter hostilities of older citizens who resented their cultures and their presence. On the frontier even upper status standing in the Old Country seldom shielded immigrants. Noel Iverson in *Germania, U.S.A.: Social Change in New Ulm, Minnesota* (Minneapolis: University of Minnesota Press, 1966), notes that conflict broke out between newcomer Germans of high Old Country status and those of ordinary standing in Germany who held that position after emigrating to America. The ethnic community had to undergo radical change to conform to the requirements of the less stratified new land, if it planned to survive.

A generation or two ago studies focused more on the affective ties of isolated ethnic communities, and some implied that affect could substitute for the many social and economic deprivations some experienced. A relatively recent compilation of excellent studies on the community in continuity and change is Robert M. French, ed., *The Community: A Comparative Perspective* (Itasca, Ill.: F. E. Peacock Publishers, Inc., 1969).

2.   Parmatma Saran, "New Ethnics: East Indians in New York City," in Roy S. Bryce-Laporte, ed., *Sourcebook on the New Immigration* (New York: Praeger, 1980).

3.   Iverson, p. 11.

4.   One can get some idea of what Boley once was by reading William Loren Katz, *The Black West: A Documentary and Pictorial History* (Garden City, N.Y.: Doubleday & Co., 1971), and Booker T. Washington, "Boley: A Negro Town in the West," ibid., 313–17. W. Sherman Savage notes that Boley was established by W. H. Boley, president of the Fort Smith and Western Railroad Townsite Company. It was a railroad town situated in Okfuskee County, where many blacks had been given land grants. The railroad employed blacks who lived in Boley. At the time of Washington's visit in 1903, Boley had two banks, two cotton mills, a newspaper, a hotel, the Creek Seminole College and Agricultural Institute, and other facilities. S. W. S. Savage, *Blacks in the West* (Westport, Conn.: Greenwood Press, Inc., 1977).

5.   Perhaps the two most informative works on Tontitown are W. J. Lemke, *The History of Tontitown, Arkansas* (Fayetteville, Ark.: Washington County Historical Society, August, 1963), and Charles T. Griffin, "Italians of Northwest Arkansas: A Sociological Analysis of Tontitown, Arkansas," (MA thesis, University of Arkansas, 1967).

6.   U.S. Department of Commerce, Bureau of the Census, *Population,* vol. 2 (1940): 419.

7.   See Joseph T. Manzo, "The Role of External Factors in the Decline of the Strawberry Hill Neighborhood," *Ethnicity* 7 (1980): 47–55, and Russell L. Gerlach, *Immigrants in the Ozarks: A Study in Ethnic Geography* (Columbia, Mo.: University of Missouri Press, 1976).

8: FROM NATIONALISM TO MANIPULATED PLURALISM

1.   Laurence J. Peter and Raymond Hull, *The Peter Principle* (New York: William Morrow & Co., Inc., 1969).

2.   Kenneth B. Clark, *Dark Ghetto* (New York: Harper & Row, 1965). See also Bettylou Valentine, *Hustling and Other Hard Work: Life Styles in the Ghetto* (Riverside, N.J.: The Free Press, 1979).

3.   The ghetto has been examined from many perspectives and found to be pathological. One of the most stinging exposés was Daniel Patrick Moynihan, *The Negro Family: The Case for National Action* (United States Department of Labor, Office of Policy, Planning, and Research, March 1965). See also Lee Rainwater, *Behind Ghetto Walls* (Chicago: Aldine Publishing Co., 1970).

4.   Thomas R. Cripps, "The Death of Rastus: Negroes in American Films since 1945," in D. G. Bromley and C. F. Longine, Jr., *White Racism and Black Americans* (Cambridge, Mass.: Schenkman Publishing Co., Inc., 1972), pp. 605–16.

5.   For an excellent summary of underlying social assumptions in black writings, see Blyden Jackson, "The Negro's Image of the Universe as Reflected in His Fiction," in ibid., pp. 628–36.

9: SEPARATISM IN THE SOCIAL SCIENCES

1.   The idea that races differ biologically goes back some time. A good overview of the issue is William Stanton, *The Leopard's Spots: Scientific Attitudes toward Race in America, 1815–59* (Chicago: University of Chicago Press, 1960).

2.   The ideas of Francis Galton, Houston Chamberlain, Lothrop Stoddard, Madison Grant, and Arthur de Gobineau, prominent men in the biological school of racism, are presented succinctly in L. C. Dunn and Theodosius Dobzhansky, *Heredity, Race and Society: A Scientific Explanation of Human Differences* (New York: New American Library, 1952), pp. 7–19.

3.   No black American emigrated to Africa as a direct result of Garvey's efforts. See Leonard Broom and Norval Glenn, *Transformation of the Negro American* (New York: Harper & Row, 1965), pp. 41–42.

4.   Bogardus began publishing his findings on social distance in 1926. His conclusion that prejudice toward ethnic groups was normative became entrenched in social science thought. See E. S. Bogardus, "Racial Distance in the United States during the Past Thirty Years," *Sociology and Social Research* 43 (1958): 127–35.

5.   That blacks who were of lighter skin had better economic and social opportunities than darker ones was standard fare in social science books until the rise of the black power movement in the 1960s. See E. F. Frazier, *The Black Bourgeoisie* (New York: Collier, 1962), for a general appreciation of this thesis.

Although there are not so many physical differences between European and American whites, correlations have seldom been made between their economic and social success and their meeting an American white standard of beauty. For instance, are taller, blond, straight-nosed Jews more successful than those with stereotypically more Jewish features? Are dark-haired Irish more successful than redheads?

6.   The conflict position is elaborated by Lewis Coser, *The Functions of Social Conflict* (New York: Free Press, 1956). The functionalist perspective is pointed out in some detail in Mark Abrahamson, *Functionalism* (Englewood Cliffs, N.J.: Prentice-Hall, 1978).

7.   William Graham Sumner, in *Folkways* (Boston: Ginn and Co., 1906), spent most of his influential book trying to prove this point by reference to many cross-cultural examples of its application.

8.   Warner presented the strongest argument on race relations as caste relations in his introduction to Allison Davis and Burleigh Gardner, *Deep South* (Chicago: University of Chicago Press, 1941).

9.   Gerald Berreman, "Caste in India and the United States," *American Journal of Sociology* 66 (September 1960): 120–27.

10.   O. C. Cox, *Caste, Class and Race* (Garden City, N.Y.: Doubleday, 1948) is probably the most closely identified with a rejection of the caste doctrine in American social relations.

NOTES / 131

11. See Bertram W. Doyle, *The Etiquette of Race Relations in the South: A Study in Social Control* (Chicago: University of Chicago Press, 1937).
12. During his lifetime Professor O. C. Cox, with whom the writer worked for some years, talked about the blocking of his professional mobility for his failure to adhere to the prevailing notion of the time that blacks and whites represented castes in America.
13. Sigmund Livingston, *Must Men Hate?* (New York: Harper & Brothers, 1944) supplies many examples of anti-Semitism being supported by fabricated data. People who hate are not likely to follow the canons of objectivity which science requires.
14. See E. O. Wilson, *Sociobiology: The New Synthesis* (Cambridge, Mass.: Harvard University Press, 1975), for one of the latest scholarly attempts to explain cultural differences on genetic bases.

10: POLITICAL AND CULTURAL PLURALISM COMPARED

1. J. S. Furnivall, *Colonial Policy and Practice* (London: Cambridge University Press, 1948), p. 304.
2. An assessment of Nkrumah's plan for Africa is found in Stanislav Andreski, *The African Predicament* (London: Michael Joseph, 1968), pp. 123–28.
3. Some idea of the vision of Lumumba in unifying the Congo (Zaire) can be read in Crawford Young, *The Politics of Cultural Pluralism* (Madison, Wis.: University of Wisconsin Press, 1976), pp. 163, 174, and 192–93.
4. See John Cohen, *Africa Addio* (New York: Ballantine Books, 1966), pp. 123–78.
5. That Kenyatta stood as a symbol of the unity of all Kenyans is evidenced in George Bennett and Carl Rosberg, *The Kenyatta Election: Kenya* (London: Oxford University Press, 1961).
6. Young, pp. 265–66.
7. See Patrick Gilkes, *The Dying Lion: Feudalism and Modernization in Ethiopia* (London: Julian Friedmann, 1974), and Marina Ottoway, *Ethiopia: Empire in Revolution* (New York: Africana Publishers, 1978).
8. The different peoples of South Africa are referred to in the official government literature as "nations." See, for example, *Progress through Separate Development: South Africa in Peaceful Transition,* 4th ed. (New York: Information Service of South Africa, 1973).
9. Elizabeth Colson, "The Assimilation of Aliens among Zambian Tonga," in Ronald Cohen and John Middleton, eds., *From Tribe to Nation in Africa: Studies in Incorporation Processes* (Scranton: Chandler Publishing Co., 1970), pp. 35–53.
10. A leading example of the primordialist argument is Harold Isaacs, *Idols of the Tribe* (New York: Harper & Row, 1977), especially "The Houses of Muumbi" and "The Snowman."
11. Robert A. Dahl and C. E. Lindblom, *Politics, Economics, and Welfare* (New York: Harper & Bros., 1953).
12. H. L. Mencken, "On Being an American," in Saul D. Feldman and Gerald W. Thielbar, *Life Styles: Diversity in American Society* (Boston: Little, Brown & Co., 1972), pp. 22–31.
13. In 1978 the Supreme Court of the United States considered the case of *Regents of the University of California* v. *Bakke.* Alan Bakke, a white man, contended he was discriminated against in applying for admission to the University of California Medical School at Davis because of his race. The court agreed with him. On the matter of race and discrimination, see Nathan Glazer, *Affirmative Discrimination: Ethnic Inequality and Public Policy* (New York: Basic Books, 1975); and Barry R. Gross, ed., *Reverse Discrimination* (Buffalo, N.Y.: Prometheus Books, 1977).

11: THE ROLE OF THE SCHOOL IN PLURALISTIC TEACHING

1. Mario Fantini, cited in William M. Cave and Mark A. Chesler, *Sociology of Education: An Anthology of Issues and Problems* (New York: Macmillan, 1974), pp. 460–61.
2. *Lau v. Nichols,* 414 U.S. 563, n. 2 (1974).
3. The ruling was by Judge Charles W. Joiner. See *Martin Luther King, Jr., Elementary School Children* v. *Ann Arbor School District Board 473,* Federal Supplement 1371, 1979.
4. U.S. Department of Health, Education and Welfare, Office of Education, Bureau of Postsecondary Education, Ethnic Heritage Studies Branch, Guidelines, p. 2.
5. Christopher Jencks, *Inequality* (New York: Basic Books, 1972).
6. See Lorenzo Middleton and William A. Sievert, "The Uneasy Undercurrent," *Chronicle of Higher Education,* May 15, 1978, and Gordon D. Morgan's letter of rebuttal, "'Uneasy Undercurrent': Relations between Blacks and Whites on Predominantly White Campuses," *Chronicle of Higher Education,* (June 19, 1978).
7. This is a term which is commonly used by academics to summarize the idea that races differ by tested intelligence. Although allegations of a strong relationship between race and I.Q. have been made before, it was probably A. R. Jensen's article "How Much can We Boost IQ and Scholastic Achievement?" *Harvard Educational Review* 39 (1969): 1–123, which began the debate anew. For another perspective on the issue see Val Woodward, "IQ and Scientific Racism," in Ann Arbor Science for the People Editorial Collective, *Biology As a Social Weapon* (Minneapolis, Minn.: Burgess Publishing Co., 1977), pp. 37–55.

12: CULTURAL PLURALISM: The Development of an Idea and a Concept

1. The ethnicist Andrew Greeley places self-hatred at the end of the American acculturation process. Assimilated former ethnics hate themselves for their non-ethnic emphasis. See Charles F. Marden and Gladys Meyer, *Minorities in American Society,* 3rd ed. (New York: American Book Co., 1969), pp. 179–220.
2. See Robert A. Dahl and C. E. Lindblom, *Politics, Economics and Welfare* (New York: Harper & Bros., 1953), where the definition of political pluralism is presented. The idea is that pluralism provides checks and balances, thus keeping the system in equilibrium. This position is commonly called the democratic view of political pluralism.
3. C. W. Mills, *The Power Elite* (New York: Oxford University Press, 1956), sees a political power structure, national in scope, made up of corporate, military, and governmental elites.
4. J. S. Furnivall, *Colonial Policy and Practice* (London: Cambridge University Press, 1948), p. 304, and in Crawford Young, *The Politics of Cultural Pluralism* (Madison, Wisconsin: The University of Wisconsin Press, 1976), p. 17.
5. M. G. Smith, "Social Structure in the British Caribbean about 1820," *Social and Economic Studies* 1, no. 4 (1953): 55–79.
6. M. G. Smith, "Social and Cultural Pluralism," in Vera Rubin, ed., *Social and Cultural Pluralism in the Caribbean,* Annals of the New York Academy of Sciences no. 83 (January 1960), pp. 763–77.
7. George Ritzer, K. C. W. Kammeyer, and N. R. Yetman, *Sociology Experiencing a Changing Society* (Boston: Allyn and Bacon, 1979), p. 337.
8. Crawford Young, *The Politics of Cultural Pluralism* (Madison, Wis.: University of Wisconsin Press, 1976).
9. Cynthia Enloe, *Ethnic Conflict and Political Development* (Boston: Little, Brown & Co., 1973), p. 15.

10. Grace DeSantis and Richard Benkins, "Ethnicity without Community," *Ethnicity* 7 (1980): 137–43.
11. Ibid.
12. Tom W. Smith, "Ethnic Measurement and Identification," *Ethnicity* 7 (1980): 78–95. A very penetrating and scholarly critique of the pluralistic logic is Orlando Patterson, *Ethnic Chauvinism: The Reactionary Impulse* (New York: Stein and Day, 1977).
13. Geneva Smitherman, professor of linguistics at Wayne State University, Detroit, Michigan, is pressing for recognition of Black English. See *Arkansas Gazette,* July 18, 1978, p. 4B.
14. See Studs Terkel interview with C. P. Ellis, "Why I Quit the Klan," *Southern Exposure,* 8, no. 2 (Summer 1980): 95–100.

13: THE DEPLURALIZATION OF BLACKS AND OTHER GROUPS

1. See in D. R. Colburn and George E. Pozzetta, *America and the New Ethnicity* (New York: Kennikat Press, 1979), p. 130.
2. A leading proponent of primordialism is Harold Isaacs. See his *Idols of the Tribe: Group Identity and Political Change* (New York: Colophon Editions, Harper & Row, 1977).

CONCLUDING REMARKS

1. See Edna Bonacich, "A Theory of Ethnic Antagonism: The Split-Labor Market," *American Sociological Review* 37 (October 1972): 547–59, "Advanced Capitalism and Black-White Relations in the U.S.: A Split-Labor Market Interpretation," *American Sociological Review* 41 (February 1976): 34–51, and "Abolition, the Extension of Slavery and the Position of Free Blacks: A Study of Split-Labor Markets in the U.S., 1830–1863," *American Journal of Sociology* 81 (November 1975): 601–28.
2. See Stephan Thernstrom, ed., *Harvard Encyclopedia of American Ethnic Groups* (Cambridge, Mass.: Belknap Press of Harvard University Press, 1980), for the latest evidence of academic interest in the revival of ethnicity.

INDEX

Charles, Ray, 72
Cherokee Nation, 58
Chesler, Mark A., 132
Chicano(s), 38, 97, 117
Chinatown, 64
Chinese, 103
Chinoy, E., 102
Civil War, 36, 42, 45, 57, 80, 118, 120
Clark, K. B., 126, 129
Cleaver, Eldridge, 65
Cohen, John, 131
Cohen, Ronald, 131
Colburn, David R., 128, 133
Coleman, James, 6, 40
Coleman, William, 48
Colonialism, 36
Colson, Elizabeth, 84, 131
Comer, James P., 26, 27, 126
Compromise of 1877, 42
Congo, 84
Cooley, Charles H., 28
Coser, Lewis, 28, 130
Cox, O. C., 37, 127, 128, 130, 131
Crèvecoeur, 23
Cripps, Thomas R., 70, 129, 130
Cubans, 117
Cuber, J., 102
Cultural homogeneity, 101
Cultural pluralism, 19
Cultural relativity, 101
Czechs, 92

Dahl, Robert A., 85, 103, 131, 132
Danes, 57, 63
D'Antonio, W., 103
Darendorf, Ralf, 28
Davis, Allison, 130
Davis, Benjamin O., Sr., 32
Davis, J. F., 127
Davis, John, Senator, 13
Defleur, L. R., 103
Defleur, M. L., 103
Deloria, Vine, Jr., 29, 30, 31, 127
Depluralization, 110, 114
DeSantis, Grace, 107, 133
Dewey, John, 20
Dobzhansky, Theodosius, 130
Douglas, J., 103
Doyle, Bertram W., 131
DuBois, W. E. B., 119
Dunbar, Paul Lawrence, 70
Dunn, L. C., 130
Durkheim, E., 108
Dutch, 44, 57, 63

Elementary and Secondary Act of
  1965, 93
Ellis, C. P., 133
Ellison, Ralph, 70
English, 89, 91, 92
Enloe, Cynthia, 106, 132
Epps, Edgar G., 22, 25, 26, 126
Essien-Udom, E. U., 74, 75
Ethnic community, 56
Ethnic Heritage Studies Program, 93
Ethnocentrism, 98
Evolutionists, 99
Exodusters, 57

Fairchild, Henry, 22
Fantini, Mario, 132
Faris, R. E. L., 102
Fascism, 89, 90
Feldman, Saul D., 131
Flemish, 44
Franklin, J. H., 119
Frazier, E. Franklin, 119, 127, 130
French, 53, 59, 89
French, Robert M., 129
Forsyth, J. M., 35, 37, 127
Furnivall, J. S., 83, 103, 131, 132
Fruchtbaum, Harold, 20, 126

Galton, Francis, 130
Gardner, Burleigh, 130
Garvey, Marcus, 36, 66, 70, 74, 75, 115
Garveyism, 96
Gerlach, Russell L., 129
German(s), 57, 60, 61, 62, 63, 113, 123
Ghana, 84
Gibson, Kenneth, 118
Giddings, Franklin H., 49, 128
Gilkes, Patrick, 131
Glazer, Nathan, 6, 17, 39, 76, 100, 108,
  112, 126, 131
Glenn, Norval, 130
Gobineau, Arthur de, 130
Goffman, E., 50, 129
Gordon, Milton, 13, 103, 104, 125, 128
Gouldner, A., 102
Gouldner, H. P., 102
Grant, Madison, 14, 22, 130
Gravely, Samuel, 48
Great Depression, 36
Green, A., 102
Greenberg, E. S., 127
Greek(s), 64, 110, 114
Greeley, Andrew, 35, 76, 101, 132
Griffin, Charles T., 129